The Making of a Radical

The life and times of Thomas Bacon (1754-1831)
Working class radical from Pentrich
'Nestor' of Derbyshire'

> Achilles: "The prize I am giving you has no relation to the Sports."
> Nestor: "Now, I must leave this sort of thing to younger men and take the painful lessons of Old Age to heart."
> (Homer's Odyssey.1178 BC)

by

Michael Parkin

First published in 2015

Other Books by the same author:

Historical

"1817 A Recipe for Revolution" (2014) ISBN 9781500770266
Causes of the 1817 Pentrich Rising

Children's Stories

"The Bravest Bear I know" (2014) ISBN 9781500877637
The story of a teddy bear experiencing The Great War.
Suitable for 9 – 15 years

"Hector's Rescue" (2014) ISBN 9781402427045
Suitable for 4 – 9 years

All available on Amazon.

© Michael Parkin 2015

All rights reserved. No part of this publication may be reproduced, stored in a retrieval system, or transmitted in any form, or by any means, electronic, mechanical, photocopying, recording or otherwise, without the prior permission of the copyright holder.

Thomas Bacon as 'Nestor'

In Greek mythology, Nestor was an Argonaut, who, amongst other feats, helped fight the centaurs and was often sought after for advice.

Homer's characterization of Nestor is not without subtle humour. In the Iliad, Nestor's advice in any given situation is often given only after he has first, somewhat garrulously displaying his vanity, spent several minutes explaining his own heroic conduct in the past when faced with similar circumstances.

Homer offers contradictory portrayals of Nestor as a source of advice. On one hand, Homer describes him as a wise man; Nestor repeatedly offers advice. Yet at the same time Nestor's advice is frequently ineffective. Yet Nestor is never questioned and instead is frequently praised.

The characters in the Iliad ignore the discrepancy between the quality of Nestor's advice and its outcomes because, "outcomes are ultimately in the hands of the ever arbitrary and fickle gods ... heroes are not necessarily viewed as responsible when things go awry." Therefore Nestor should be viewed as a good counsellor because of the qualities he possesses as a man of "sweet words," a "clear-voiced orator," and whose voice "flows sweeter than honey." These are elements that make up Nestor, and they parallel the elements that Homer describes as part of a good counsellor.

Nestor is a good counsellor inherently, and the consequences of his advice have no bearing on that, a view that differs from how good counsellors are viewed today.

Contents

    Chronology 1
1. Preface 3
2. A Journey through a Lifetime... 7
3. The Making of a Radical 11
    The domestic man 11
    Enclosures 12
    An elementary education 14
    The working man 15
4. Radical Influences 22
    John Wilkes (1725–1797).. 24
    Thomas Paine (1737-1809) 24
    Edmund Burke (1729-1797) 26
    William Cobbett (1763-1835).. 28
    Major John Cartwright (1740-1824) 31
    Sir Francis Burdett (1770-1844) 34
    William Benbow (1784-1841) 35
    Samuel Bamford (1788-1872) 36
    Thomas Wooler (1786-1853) 36
    Gravener Henson (1785–1852).. 37
    Thomas Spence (1750-1814).. 39
5. Radicalising Tommy 41
    A Three-Cornered Hat... 46
    The Impact of Religion... 47
6. Visiting America 50
7. Luddites and the Rest 55
    Origins of the 'Luddites' 56
    Local Law Enforcement 60

8.	Radical Societies	63
	Early Societies	63
	The London Corresponding Society	63
	Origins of the Hampden Clubs	65
	'Second Generation' Hampden Clubs	67
	Secret Committees	69
9.	Growing Discontent	71
	A Dangerous Mix	72
	A Developing Situation	73
	The Spa Fields Riots, 2 December 1816	74
10.	The Crown and Anchor, London	78
11.	International Distractions	83
	American War of Independence	83
	The Irish Problem	84
	French Revolution	85
12.	Legislation	87
	Protection of Stocking Frames, etc. Act 1788	87
	The Treason Act 1790	88
	Habeas Corpus	88
	The Seditious Meetings Act 1795	89
	The Treason Act 1795	90
	Unlawful Oaths Act 1797	90
	Unlawful Societies Act 1799	90
	Combination Act 1799	91
	Combination Act 1800	91
	Health and Morals of Apprentices Act 1802	91
	Watch and Ward (Luddites) Act 1812	92
	The Destruction of Stocking Frames, etc. (Frame Breaking) Act 1812	92

    Importation Act 1815 93

    Habeas Corpus Suspension Act 1817 93

    Treason Act 1817 94

    Seditious Meetings Act 1817 94

    The "Six Gagging Acts" 95

13.   What about the Women? 97

14.   1817 Meetings 102

    Nottingham Secret Committee 103

    Delegates' Meetings 104

    Asherfield Farm Meetings 106

    Bacon and Butterley Company 106

    Deposition of Armond Booth 108

    Deposition of John Cope 111

    Change of Date 112

    Meeting Dates 113

15.   London Packet & Lloyd's Evening News 3rd Nov 1817 114

    What the Revolutionaries Wanted 114

    The Abstract 115

    Cannon and Pikes at Butterley 115

    Nottingham to be the Capital 116

    A New Bank and a New Coinage 117

    Brandreth to Command 118

16.   Tommy Goes Missing 120

17.   The Rising 125

    The Death of Robert Walker 126

    Mr Goodwin and Butterley Company 127

    Onwards and Upwards 128

    Towards the End 129

18.	The Huddersfield Story	131
19.	The Trials	135
	Pre-Trial Processes	135
	The Trials Begin	138
	The Sentencing	138
	Bacon's Guilty Plea	140
20.	After the Trial	142
	Life in Australia	145
21.	Reflections of a Radical	147
22.	Conclusions	151
	John Stevens' Concluding Comments	151
Bibliography		159
Index		160

Chronology

This chronology of the key events during Thomas Bacon's life should not be seen as exhaustive mainly because I have only included the matters that could conceivably have had an impact on his life and his developing radical activities. At the very least, I hope it provides a framework for the story and multitude of time-consuming pressures on working people, the Monarch and his government during this period.

Born in **1754,** baptised at St Matthew's Church, Pentrich on 25th Dec 1754.
1756 to **1763** Britain at war with France
1760 Death of George II, George III Crowned
1769 Arkwright's water power and Watts Steam power both patented
1770 Hargreaves Spinning Jenny patented
1773 Boston Tea Party, protests against British rule and taxation in America
1774 to **1783** America's war of Independence
1775 / 1776 Hundreds of Arkwright's frames smashed in England
1775 Thomas Bacon 21 years of age, working as a framework knitter
1777 to **1789** limited period of impressment to British army
1780 Gordon Riots, originally anti-Catholic but developed into general disturbances
1785 Daily Universal Register (now *The Times*) launched
1788 The *Derby Mercury* newspaper was re-launched after being Drewry's *Derby Mercury* from **1732**
1788 George III's first serious illness
1789 English sailors Mutiny on HMS Bounty
1789 to **1799** French Revolution
1790 Burke's Reflections on the French Revolution published
1791 Paine's *Right of Man Part 1* published in France
1792 London Corresponding Society Formed
1792 Paine's *Right of Man Part 2* arrives in England
1793 to **1815** War with France (temporary halt in **1802**)
1795 Food Riots around England
1795 Speenhamland poor relief system introduced

1796 Spain joins in with war against Britain
1798 Irish Rebellion
1799 First Combination Act
1799 British Army in Holland surrenders
1800 Thomas Bacon 46 years of age
1800 Second Combination Act
1801 Ireland becomes part of UK
1802 Trevithick's steam road engine launched
1802 Cobbett's *Political Register* first published
1805 Battle of Trafalgar
1802 Formal abolition of Slave Trade
1808 Start of Peninsular War
1809 Thomas Paine died
1810 to **1814** main period of Luddite activity mainly in Midlands and North of England
1811 George III finally declared insane and Regency period began
1812 Lord Byron's maiden speech giving some support to working classes
1812 to **1815** Anglo-American War
1815 Poor harvest in Britain
1815 Mount Tambora eruption thought to have impacted on weather
1816 Another poor harvest in Britain, snow during June in Buxton
1816 Cobbett's *Address to Labourers* published
1816 2nd Dec Spa Fields Riots in London
1817 January meeting at Crown and Anchor, London
1817 24th February Habeas Corpus suspended
1817 10th March 'Blanketeers March' from Manchester
1817 9th June Pentrich Rising
1817 Thomas Bacon was 63 years of age
1817 Trials at Derby
1817 7th November Executions at Derby
1818 Transportations to Australia
1819 Peterloo Massacre in Manchester
1820 29th January Prince Regent became George IV on death of George III
1823 Death Penalty abolished for more than 100 crimes
1824 Combination Acts of 1799 and 1800 repealed
1831 Died, age 77, at Port Macquarie, New South Wales, Australia

1. Preface

After the publication of my book, *'1817 A Recipe for Revolution'*, I retained the curiosity and enthusiasm to delve a little deeper into the particular version of radicalism demonstrated by one of the Pentrich Rising leaders, Thomas Bacon. Although, for a variety of reasons I will explore later, he did not, in actual fact, take part in the Rising but chose to sit it out alone in a secluded hovel close to the village of Pentrich in central Derbyshire. He absented himself on the day before the Rising he had been instrumental in planning; this was an odd decision that may well have been crucial in saving his life!

However, it is generally accepted that he was intensely involved in the heightened political awareness and amplified emotions of the working men in his locality and even wider afield. In the years leading up to the Rising, he was also heavily enmeshed in radical agitation and in the organisation of the Rising itself. As the 'Derbyshire Delegate' in the build up to the planned insurrection, he had a high profile in other regions and was listed as a 'delegate' to many of the key meetings, particularly in 1816 and 1817. To these ends he travelled extensively throughout England. At the time of the Rising in mid-1817, he had been undoubtedly the main instigator of insurrection in his area of central Derbyshire and had been so for almost thirty years. At a time when the working class was emerging as a recognised group and in parallel with the progression of the industrial revolution he was definitely a man of his time!

Using the standard dictionary definition of '**radical**' as a noun we find *'a person who favours extreme or fundamental change in existing institutions or in political, social or economic conditions'*. This certainly encompasses the political ambitions of Thomas Bacon. It also embraces the position of several national figures who influenced Bacon throughout his life such as Thomas Paine, William Cobbett, Major John Cartwright, Henry 'Orator' Hunt and others. However, Bacon expounded views that would take radicalism further than the desire for parliamentary reform by 'legal methods' publically demanded by most of these men – he would, if given the chance, seek to bring about change by more unconstitutional means.

Anyone interested in the Pentrich Rising will doubtless begin their studies by reading John Neal's *"The Pentrich Revolution"*[1] and John Stevens' *"England's Last Revolution – Pentrich 1817"*[2]; both excellent pieces of work. In fact, John Neal wrote his original articles for publication in local newspapers towards the end of the nineteenth century and was able to speak to some of the direct descendants and even a few survivors of the Rising. I will make several references to these books throughout my text and I would take this opportunity of expressing my thanks for their creditable work.

In seeking references to Thomas Bacon and his times, I resorted to other well-known texts covering this period such as White's *"Waterloo to Peterloo"*. These and other relevant books will be acknowledged as they arise and sources used together with suggestions for further reading are included in the bibliography.

If any reader is seeking a wider perspective of this period and the relationship between the industrial revolution and the development of the working class, I can direct you to no better place than the outstanding book by E.P. Thompson, *"The Making of the Working Class"* originally published in 1963 and later in paperback by Penguin. Thompson delves deeply into the developing working class in the contexts of industrial changes, the impact of religion, particularly Methodism; he also dissects the Luddite movement and takes the story forward from where we leave it at Bacon's death to the Reform Act 1832.

The saga of the Pentrich Rising is central to the wider story of the Industrial Revolution both from the perspective of time (agreed by most historians to be 1750 to 1850) and location. The area around Pentrich (occasionally given the ancient name of *"Pentridge"* in some text books) in central Derbyshire provided the back-drop to the Rising by being located in the centre of the industrial revolution as it was in 1817. This includes the early growth of industrialisation and the development of powered factories.

---

[1] Neal, John, (1966) "The Pentrich Revolution" Pentrich Church Restoration Committee (originally published as newspaper articles in 1895
[2] Stevens, John, (1977) "England's Last Revolution" Moorland Publishing, Buxton

The first factory was built by Lombe in Derby Silk Mill[3] in 1717, and the significant local development by Arkwright and Strutt were close by in Ambergate (1771) and Belper (1786) respectively.

The area was strongly represented by framework knitters weaving wool garments, including the famous Derbyshire Rib stockings and, until the late eighteenth century, based at their homes. The advance in industrial methods, particularly the introduction of water and later steam power, and the greater availability of imported cotton changed the context of the area. Cotton had been used as early as the sixteenth century but its availability increased during Bacon's time. It was particularly suited to mass production factory methods.

Researching a life lived some 200 and more years ago can be problematic. It is even more so when that life is spent exclusively in the lowest echelons of society where written records are virtually unknown. I suspect that Bacon was a man who would not wish to have all his activities and opinions logged. He never held a formal position of authority or status nor did he, as far as we know, commit his works and thoughts to a diary, journal or autobiography. There are no published papers and few categorical statements of his views and opinions. Nevertheless he did influence others and he did attract a degree of respect way beyond the village of Pentrich. Until his transportation at the age of 64, Thomas Bacon was central to the development of radicalism in Derbyshire and beyond.

It occurs to me that Bacon would spin in his unmarked grave in Port Macquarie, New South Wales, Australia should he ever become aware that someone is attempting to analyse his life; but this is precisely what I seek to do in these pages. The local history society of which I am a member meets only yards from where Thomas Bacon was born but, by most other, measures is a million miles away.

I have tried to find substance for any statements I put forward, to corroborate and, where possible, triangulate evidence supporting the

---

[3] Derby Silk Mill Museum is open daily and located in the centre of Derby.

information upon which I rely. This said much of the evidence is circumstantial, educated guesswork or downright speculation; even the veracity of some quotes that have been taken from previously published sources should be treated with extreme caution. Many of the conversations and decisions, both local and at the level of government were taken in secret and where records do exist they cannot be seen as absolutely reliable. Furthermore, statements made during the course of the trials or pre-trial depositions should be viewed with scepticism as those making them clearly have their own agenda – as do those recording them! In this regard very little seems to have changed to-day. However, there is solid corroboration of his activities in the key period of January to June 1817.

Several of the standard text books on this period contain familiar statements and quotes and some have no formal reference. This does not, of course, mean they are not true but they must be placed in context and against the limited facts of which we are sure.

However, whilst expressing my thanks for the assistance of many friends and colleagues, any errors in content or interpretation are mine alone. I would like thank my wife Sandra and Les Herbert for their help in proof-reading and providing recommendations for a readable text.

Michael Parkin
Derbyshire 2015
mparkin109@gmail.com
www.michael-parkin.uk

2. A Journey through a Lifetime

To reach the grand old age of 77 was quite an achievement in the early nineteenth century. To spend your final days in the warmth of the Australian Pacific coast is an achievement few born to rural working class stock in mid-Derbyshire would aspire to or even be aware of. Thomas Bacon did both of these; he died whilst a resident of could only be described as a 'retirement home' for aged convicts in what is now a renowned holiday region of Parramatta, New South Wales, Australia.

If the government of Lord Liverpool had been able to achieve their declared aim, Bacon would have been hanged, beheaded set alongside Brandreth, Turner and Ludlam and paraded in St Mary's Gate, Derby. However, in Derbyshire dialect, *'wick t'th'end'*, Thomas Bacon managed to get away with no more than a few months in jail and a free cruise to Australia, albeit a one-way ticket.

The story of Thomas Bacon's early years, beginning in chapter three, is predominantly speculation but follows the life a typical young person would have known in a small rural village from the middle to the end of the eighteenth century. It seems fairly certain that Thomas learnt the trade of a framework knitter, a common occupation in the area. We will trace a conventional life of a young man, although Thomas Bacon turned out to be somewhat less than conventional as were his opinions on the developing world he inhabited. We know he did not marry and we know he remained a resident of Pentrich, staying in the family home close to what is now the village hall. We also know that, by attending the local church Sunday school, he was competent in reading and writing from an early age and those skills were not given to all of his station in life.

It is most likely Thomas did become aware of politics and did internalise radical views perhaps from around the time news was spreading of the French Revolution; this was 1789 when he was 35. The events in France did raise the emotions and provoke a new agitation in various levels of English society; the English Jacobinism was undoubtedly a by-product of the Revolution. Chapter four looks at a range of people who probably influenced Bacon; some he will have read about and some he would later meet. Chapter five offers some thoughts on the radicalisation of Thomas Bacon in the context of these events.

Some of the texts describe Thomas Bacon as a veteran solider and as having visited America. Of course this was a time when many Europeans were emigrating to the New World, the slave trade was still big business and soldiers were being shipped across the Atlantic to fight in the War of Independence and other conflicts. In chapter six I attempt to analyse the evidence supporting these assertions.

Bacon was certainly an active Luddite and probably a local leader and organiser of frame-breaking. In chapter seven the Luddite period is dealt with, together with the evidence that Bacon was involved. His experiences of direct action may well have established a belief that could in fact contribute to his efforts to bring about working class revolution.

As the radical movement expanded a range of organisations, including corresponding societies, secret committees and 'political clubs', sprang up around the country. Chapter eight looks at these and Bacon's association with them.

Chapter nine looks at the growing discontentment around the country and, in particular, the midlands and north; a phenomenon the government papers named 'the Disturbances'. In chapter ten we step aside to consider the *Crown and Anchor* in London and its position in providing a centre for key meetings and a different level of radicalism.

Whilst this story is unfolding, it is worth bearing in mind the international context at the time. Britain was permanently involved in a wide range of incidents and activities around the world, many necessitating intense governmental attention and, of course, having a negative impact on the national economy. Chapter eleven sets out some of the more serious international events running concurrently with Tommy Bacon's life.

As we shall see, the government sought to squash internal disturbances, vocal dissatisfaction and challenges by those seeking change. Chapter twelve looks at the range and extent of legislation enacted for these purposes during the years immediately preceding the Pentrich Rising.

During a meeting of the *Pentrich and South Wingfield Revolution Group* earnestly planning for the 2017 bi-centenary of the Pentrich Rising, someone raised the question "I wonder what the womenfolk thought of the actions of their men?" This is, indeed, a pertinent question and ought to be addressed; in chapter thirteen I will try to shine a little light into the darkness behind closed doors.

As the plans for the Rising developed, a series of meetings where held throughout the first half of 1817 and chapter fourteen follows the build-up to what should have been the key event in Bacon's life.

In chapter fifteen an attempt will be made to make some sense of Thomas' disappearance from the scene in the hours before the event he had been so intensively involved in for many years.

The Rising itself has been described many times and I will only hover over the key points in chapter sixteen. My reasons for this apparent omission are that I covered the event in my previous book and the 'hero' of these pages, Thomas Bacon, was not there and this is his story!

Chapter seventeen abstracts some key points from the trial and, for this purpose, I use, amongst other sources, the *Report of the Whole of Proceedings under the Special Commission* printed by Sutton and Son, Bridlesmith Gate, Derby.

The period of Tommy's life immediately after the trial, his voyage to Australia, including the interesting and perhaps enlightening statements he volunteered on board the convict ship the *Tottenham* and his subsequent life in Australia will be covered by chapter eighteen.

After spending a considerable amount of time delving into Thomas Bacon's life I have internalized a little of his thought processes and, together with a degree of artistic licence, I use chapter nineteen to set out what may, or may not, have been how Thomas would have viewed his life in retrospect. However, as far as I can ascertain, he never put his life into writing. In the context of his lowly position and the events of the time, it would have been fascinating if he had done so.

Finally, I seek to arrive at some conclusions in chapter twenty. Before doing so I have taken the liberty to repeat John Stevens' concluding remarks as a comparison to my attempts to arrive at some answers and, undoubtedly, providing more questions to ponder.

3. The Making of a Radical

The domestic man

Thomas Bacon was baptised at St Matthew's Parish Church, Pentrich, in the sparsely populated area of central Derbyshire on Christmas Day 1754. His father, Thomas Bacon, a small-scale tenant farmer and his mother, Ellen Walters, were married at Pentrich Parish Church on Thursday 27th September 1753; probably followed by a celebration at the White Horse Inn. Ellen's maiden name of Walters was a common family name and her relatives were destined to reappear at several stages through Tommy's life, including the Rising itself. 1754 saw a child appear which, being the first-born, was named after his father as was the custom in those days; he was known as 'Tommy'. This name stuck for his life only enhanced by adding the title 'Owd' Tommy when it seemed appropriate to do so.

At the time of Bacon's birth Pentrich was a small working village with tiny cottages side by side and occasionally set on short streets running at 90 degrees to what is now the main road. It those days the road would have been a dirt track – maybe even an open sewer. Although by no means large, Pentrich did occupy a significant position, much more so than it does to-day. Ripley, the largest town in area to-day was much smaller than Pentrich as indeed were Swanwick and South Wingfield.

The focus of the book will remain on Thomas Bacon's life, his travels, his legitimate and his illegitimate activities and his progression from a little boy in a small Derbyshire backwater into a dedicated working class radical, republican and, according to comments at his trial, a 'rascal'. He is the hero of my story or, on reflection, is he the 'anti-hero'? It all depends on your personal perspective. Your particular interest in the period, your social class, education or political leaning will dictate your answer to this question and many other questions in the pages to follow. Tommy was either 'a man ahead of his time' or a dangerous 'trouble-causer' – the government of the day would definitely take the latter view. You will not find him a particularly lovable character but you will find him intelligent, perceptive and, until approaching the Rising, consistent; a man with a keen political compass. I can imagine him to-day reincarnated as an aged, grumpy, grey-haired Labour MP, ruing the drift from extreme left wing to centre ground politics and, whenever he got the chance, expressing his strongly held views with a strong voice and a heavy Derbyshire accent. The difference being that, in the late eighteenth and early nineteenth centuries, there were plenty willing to listen to Owd Tommy and follow his lead.

Thomas was the first of ten children, including two sets of twins; Sophia (1756), Miles (1758), Anthonietta and Anthony (1761), Nancy and Fanny (1762), John (1764), John (1765) and Hannah (1768). The family lived in a small rented cottage in the village of Pentrich, included in and surrounded by the Duke of Devonshire's estate; not too far from where the village hall now stands. The second named brother, John, was doubtless due to the demise of the first John, again, not uncommon at the time. It was this John who was with Thomas at the time of his arrest and they were also transported together.

The village housing stock was mainly one or two story cottages, stone built and most with thatched roofs. There were at least two public houses, the White Horse and the Dog Inn, only the latter remains to this day. The village had a few small retailers, a blacksmiths and a butchers shop. The villages of South Wingfield, Swanwick, Ripley and Alfreton are all within walking distance.

Enclosures

During his early years, Thomas may well have noticed the domestic pressure on his parents caused by the Enclosure of common land. This is the process which ended traditional rights such as mowing meadows for hay, or grazing livestock on common land formerly held in the open field system. Once enclosed, these uses of the land become restricted to the owner, and it ceased to be land for common use. It had, for many years, been a benefit for rural workers and important in enhancing their meagre income. Some historians have suggested that this was at least partially responsible for peasants leaving the countryside to work in the town or city in industrial factories. As a small-scale farmer Tommy's father would not be well paid but they would doubtless benefit from milk, eggs, fresh chickens and the like.

The women folk (see chapter thirteen), if not fully occupied by delivering and rearing children, were expected to contribute in whatever way they could. Before the creation of jobs in factories and coal mines, many unmarried girls would work as servants and child-minders. Families were usually large by the standards of to-day but infant mortality was very high until the late 1800's.

Tommy's sister Nancy, two years younger, was to play a supportive role throughout his life. She eventually ran 'The White Horse' after her husband, one of the Weightman's, died. Many of the local planning meetings for the Rising were to be held there; she did not take part in the march herself but undoubtedly encouraged others to do so. According to all accounts, she was also openly critical of customers expressing an opinion contrary to that of 'our Tommy'. Her public house, the White Horse, was later to be the meeting room of the Pentrich Hampden Club prior to the Rising. It seems quite clear that Nancy, or as she grew older 'Nanny' Weightman supported her brother and ensured that any pertinent comment made in his absence would be faithfully reported back to him. However, she was to lose her licence, as many lost their homes, after the Rising.

A feature of the area worthy of mentioning at this early stage is the complex inter-relationships between the families in the surrounding villages. Many of the residents in Pentrich, South Wingfield and adjacent settlements such as Swanwick, Ripley, Alfreton, etc. were related, directly or indirectly by marriage. In fact, and if I jump some 50 odd years ahead in my story, of the close on 400 men who took part at some stage in the Pentrich Rising in 1817, only three were not related to any other participant; Jeremiah Brandreth, the *'Nottingham Captain'* being one of the three. Family names such as Bacon, Booth, Elliott, Ensor, Fletcher, Hall, Ludlam, Moore, Taylor, Turner, Walker, Walters and Weightman were strongly represented – and are still to be found to this day.

When not working, young Tommy and his friends and siblings would explore the fields around the village and the adjacent tracks. On several occasions Tommy would stand and watch the coaches of the wealthy trundle along the sludgy rutted turnpike at Buckland Hollow below the village and, occasionally, catch a sight of the Duke and his entourage on their way to or from Chatsworth House, only fifteen or so miles away. Their finery and comfort would seem a million miles from the life of his mother and father. It was even rumoured that Dick Turpin trod that same route whilst following his *'trade'*. It is still believed to-day that he stayed at the Peacock Coaching Inn at Oakerthorpe some 3 or 4 miles away. This story would have excited a bright lad like Tommy!

As he grew up he perhaps met some of the tinkers, drovers and pack-mule men who plied their business along the turnpike. They would deviate into Pentrich and South Wingfield selling their wares and telling their tales before heading to villages, towns and cities north and south. One or two of the villages may have been soldiers with tales to tell.

Childhood was short and not so sweet in those times, probably no more than five or seven years before starting work or charged with looking after younger siblings. As the oldest and with a mother pregnant most years Thomas would have child-care duties from an early age and until the next in line took over, in his case his sister Nancy.

An elementary education

It would be over a century, in fact to the time of the Elementary Education Act of 1870, before basic schooling became compulsory. Tommy was fortunate in that he lived close to the local parish church at Pentrich where a Sunday school for the children of the village would be held. At least, this kept the children out of trouble on the one and only rest day from work. The main and probably only textbook would be the Bible. The curriculum started with learning to read and then progressed to the catechism, a fixed question and answer format recited by rote as laid out in the Common Book of Prayer. A bright lad, Tommy apparently took to reading with little effort. Interestingly, it was many years before the schools routinely taught children how to write. It was considered unnecessary for the lower orders and, maybe by some, dangerous so to do. Whilst other books, pamphlets and newspapers were in existence they were expensive and uncommon in villages like Pentrich during the 1750's and 1760's.

However, the general maxim of education, mainly religious instruction, was *'to fit them for good servants, to endeavour as early as possible to inure them to labour, early rising and cleanliness'*. The Church would doubtless add the requirement that they must remain content with their position in life and not aspire to any higher station in life. From the perspective of Thomas Bacon's later life it would be fair to assume he did not take this entreaty to heart.

It would be around this time when some were being exposed to the sermons of travelling Methodists, adherents to John Wesley, many of whom revealed sympathy for the interests and dreams of working people. There was a Methodist chapel in Pentrich village and another at Buckland Hollow, less than a mile away.

The working man

Many of the men in Pentrich were home-based, self-employed framework knitters and weavers, the rest would be farm workers and a few following specific trades like blacksmiths, leather workers, butchers, builders and a few miners. Although there would be several mines, it should be remembered that large scale mining had not yet taken off as the major source of employment in the village at this time as the development of powered pumps was in its infancy and the risk of flooding in deep mines was a recurring threat. Mining would not overtake weaving trades as the main source of employment in this area until the first half of the nineteenth century.

It was probably with a neighbour or one of his many relatives that at the age of six or seven Tommy began to work long hours learning his trade as a framework knitter. They were frequently given the nickname 'shiners' due to the shine on the backside of their trousers after hours sliding alone on a wooden frame bench. The trade was organised in a simple manner during the mid to late eighteenth century in the period before factories took over much of the whole process. Few men would own their own knitting frame, most would rent them from a master hosier who would also supply the yarn and take the finished articles, stockings, underclothes and, occasionally, gloves to market in return for a payment, usually set on the market conditions. Messrs Brettle and Ward of Belper were one of the larger master hosiers in the area.

It was normal for framework knitters to be paid in cash and not in 'truck' (in goods or vouchers at a shop owned by the master). The 'truck' was more common during the nineteenth century in the mining industry. The actual contact between the framework knitter and the master hosier would often be via a 'putter-out' who would act as a middle-man. Some of these middle-men took an enterprising position and worked with several master hosiers and they were called 'bag hosiers'. Although it is not recorded, one can imagine Thomas Bacon finding fault with this method of exploiting the working man, he would doubtless hear the men of the village bemoaning the situation but, as ever, being powerless to do anything about it.

At the time Thomas Bacon began his working life framework knitters would be working, almost exclusively, with wool which would be readily available in Derbyshire. It was not until later when cotton began to be used extensively in weaving that some knitting, like the Derbyshire Rib Stocking, lost favour.

A few framework knitters took on apprentices placed by the local parish being responsible for the welfare of 'paupers'. The term 'apprentice' is perhaps somewhat grander than reality as these 'trainees', often orphans or illegitimate children, where paid a pittance if at all and, in many cases, not treated too well. See chapter twelve for comments on the Health and Morals of Apprentices Act 1802 which did seek to make some redress.

The work of the framework knitter was hard and hours were long but in the second half of the eighteenth century the pay, in comparison with some other trades, was quite good. Although there were difficult years, by the turn of the century some framework knitters were earning between 14s and 15s per week (75p-80p). However, worse times were ahead, by 1819, stockingers were earning 4s to 7s (20p -35p) for up to eighteen hours a day, six days a week, due to excessive supply over demand, changes in fashion, more cotton weaving and the impact of readily available power and technical developments in factories. It should be remembered that trouble and pressure within the home-based weaving trades began towards the end of the 1700's and this form of working had virtually disappeared by the 1820's.

By way of illuminating Tommy's life, most working class children would start working at some point between 6 and 9 years of age. The men would operate the machines whilst the women and children would be engaged seaming stockings, stitching ends and winding threads. Young children would be given the tedious and dangerous task of scrambling around the floor retrieving needles, loose threads and dislodged spindles. As the industrial revolution progressed a similar pattern was established in the factories but a key difference was that, whilst there were ample employment opportunities for women and children, the skilled men operated several machines and less of them were needed. Any fall in demand for the products did, of course, hit the self-employed home-worker before the mill employee. Although with employment law being practically non-existent and that which was in place being seldom enforced, the employer could lay-off his employees with impunity and, of course, often did.

This was real source of discontent and many were to advocate and undertake direct action. This plus the import of cheap material and changes in demand, particularly the fall in demand for the Derbyshire Rib stocking would ultimately lead to limited disruption and some frame-breaking by the time Bacon was in his twenties.

To make things even more difficult as factory employment became more common, it was a fact that many men found the strict regimentation of the factory hard to accept. It had been a long standing tradition that the alcoholic indulgences of Sunday evening would be resolved by a lie-in on 'Saint Monday'; this did not match the requirements of a factory where power was provided and needed to be used to its fullest extent.

The boys who demonstrated some degree of ability would progress to operating a machine from the age of 10 to 12. This would appear to have been the pattern of Thomas Bacon's early life. As a tenant farmer, his father would not be well-off but the large family would be able to contribute and the benefits of a rural life, for example a small garden left after enclosure, would suggest a relatively comfortable living within the standards of the time. However, there were considerable variations in demand for both agricultural labourers and framework knitters and their incomes over the year.

Many of the men taking part in the Pentrich Rising lived in the villages of Pentrich or South Wingfield or close by in Swanwick. It is certain that they would have been living hand-in-glove with each other throughout their childhood, adolescence and working life. Everyone knew everyone else!

When one examines the list of participants on the Rising it is clear that very few were over 50 and Thomas Bacon, who was 64 at the time of the Rising, would have been very much an 'elder statesman', to put no finer point on it – an old man! Doubtless many of the friends of his childhood died before the Rising or retired from work and were patently too old to take any practical part. As we shall see, Tommy found his own reasons for opting out of the Rising.

It seems certain he was a Pentrich resident until, in 1818, he took up involuntary domicile at His Majesty's pleasure in Australia. We do not have the benefit of a 'house by house' census until 1841 and precise detail of his time as a young man is not available. The cottage in which he lived with his parents was doubtless rented and the rental may well have been passed on the eldest son, Thomas, at some stage. It is believed his father died in the 1790's.

Other than his baptism, there are no specific records of Tommy's young life and it would have been highly unusual if there were. He was the first-born to a tenant farmer and his wife; he would have been expected to find a wife from Pentrich or close by, to rear a large family and die in the same village. The average life expectancy in 1801 was between 36 and 37 years[4]. Thomas Bacon's life was not to follow that average pattern.

Of course, a term like 'life expectancy' can be misleading; it represents an average that is heavily influenced by the high level of child mortality at the time, both still-born and those dying in their early years. This said many working men died in their fifties.

Thomas spent some time working at Butterley Company as a fettler (filing off rough edges from castings) but was dismissed for his 'radical' beliefs, his internal agitation over wage rates and, presumably, his absence whilst attending political meetings. Both these statements are feasible and 'in character' but are they true? Butterley Company was founded in 1790, when Bacon would have been 36, and grew over the next decade. It was not an unreasonable time for a career change bearing mind the pressures on framework knitters. The opening of the company would doubtless offer plenty of employment opportunities in the area. It was not, however, to last for Thomas! This may, by the way, have been his first acquaintance with the manager Mr. George Goodwin. It would be Mr Goodwin who, when giving evidence, was to label Thomas Bacon a 'rascal' and a known radical leader.

There are a great many sources verifying Bacon's travels around England, including meetings in London, particularly in the years immediately preceding the Rising. He is known to have visited and met radical delegates in Sheffield, Huddersfield, Manchester, Birmingham and Nottingham. This was highly unusual for men of his station in life and, in the years

---

[4] Gault, Hugh (2009) "1809: Between Hope and History" Gretton Brooks, Cambridge

immediately prior to the Rising, would undoubtedly have raised suspicions with local officials and local informants feeding the demands for intelligence. With the exception of carriers, gypsies, drovers and miscellaneous traders, men of Thomas Bacon's station in life seldom travelled far and, if they did, they walked. It is highly likely that the local JP, Col. Halton, knew of Thomas Bacon's activities.

There are questions to be asked about how Bacon managed to finance his lifestyle during the years 1811 to 1817. We will consider his Luddite activities in chapter seven and his 'political work' towards the end of this period. It is recorded that he sold stockings from time to time, even selling a few pairs to William Oliver the spy! However, as we shall see, he was generously supported by the locals and he did not have the responsibility of a wife and family.

Many of the locals readily gave pennies to finance Bacon's travels from meeting to meeting but how did he feed himself? Perhaps he was supported by his extended family or his sister Nancy the pub landlady? The fact that he appeared to live in the Pentrich and South Wingfield area with no visible means of support was not perhaps a situation that early writers thought worth commenting on. For me it is significant and, arguably, goes some way to indicate the status he had in his community and the manner in which many were willing to contribute to his travels. This is especially the case when one remembers that, in his sixties; he would have been seen as an 'old man'. In fact, many of the delegates at meeting used the term –old man' to identify Bacon.

There were, of course, others in the same area who developed radical views and were key players in the Luddite movement and the Pentrich Rising. They all seem to be happy to take a subordinate position to that of Thomas Bacon and most of them were many years younger than he was. If the assertion that Bacon began his serious radical views and activities around 1790/92 is true, many men would grow up to regard him as the venerable leader – the Nestor of Derbyshire.

However, before this stage, the question running through this story is how and when Thomas Bacon became a serious radical? When and how did he accrue the knowledge and awareness necessary to form and be able to articulate these views? Who and what were his early influences?

4. Radical Influences

Whether there was a specific local or national incident or epiphany, 'a moment of sudden and great revelation or understanding'[5] will never be really clear. We do know that Bacon was literate and that newspapers were beginning to be circulated, for example the *Derby Mercury* was published from 1732 and others from the 1720's, The *Times* began in 1785. In fact the first newspaper was the *Daily Courant* published first in 1702 and continued under various titles until September 1797. However, this latter publication would not have reached Pentrich! But many late eighteenth century newspapers undoubtedly would have.

Throughout Thomas Bacon's early life newspapers and political pamphlets would be circulated by travellers and read to those unable to read themselves at meetings and in public houses. He would likely have been exposed to these sources from his later teens, perhaps early 1770's. Some non-conformist religious groups followed a similar track. Bacon may have heard some inspirational speakers at the Methodist Chapels

The Peacock Inn and The Anchor at Oakerthorpe were popular coaching stopovers not too far from Pentrich and South Wingfield. One can certainly imagine the inquisitive Thomas Bacon frequenting such a place, or the Devonshire Arms at Buckland Hollow, where a great many interesting people would spend their stop-over time regaling fellow travellers and drinkers in the public bars. Many would leave newspapers or political pamphlets available for those who could to read and Thomas Bacon would doubtless gather such literature.

As a young, single man, one can imagine Thomas spending time in his sister's pub the White Horse where his reading and writing skills would be in demand. It was quite usual at this time for those who were competent to read newspapers to the locals.

---

[5] Oxford Dictionary

It may be useful to outline some of the personalities who may have influenced Bacon as a young man. In the following pages I will attempt to analysis when Bacon developed his deeply-held radical views.

Before looking at some of the contemporary reformers and radicals, I would like to include a few words about John Bunyan, author and dissenting preacher, who lived from 1628 to 1688. Having spent several periods in prison for preaching without a licence, Bunyan wrote *The Pilgrim's Progress* in two parts, the first of which was published in London in 1678 and the second in 1684. He conceived the work during his first period of imprisonment, and probably finished it during the second. The earliest edition in which the two parts were combined into one volume came in 1728. A third part – attributed to Bunyan – appeared in 1693, and was reprinted as late as 1852. Its full title is *The Pilgrim's Progress from This World to That Which Is to Come.*

The Pilgrim's Progress is arguably one of the most widely known allegories[6] ever written, and has been extensively translated. Thompson[7] suggested that Bunyan's *Pilgrim's Progress* and Paine's *The Rights of Man* were standard texts and influences of the working class radical movement. These books, which were widely available, contributed significantly to the stock of ideas and attitudes. Was *Pilgrim's Progress* part of the raw material of the Pentrich and South Wingfield radical/reform movement from 1790 to 1850?

Some elements of the radical movement were stimulated by the centenary, in 1788, of the Glorious Revolution of 1688 when James II was replaced by William and Mary. Not least of these was the public *"Take Your Pick"* by Major Cartwright in 1776. In 1789 the centenary of the Glorious Revolution was also being celebrated in Britain by two types of clubs: the Revolution Societies and the Reform Clubs. Both of these organisations attempted to assist the French with what was seen as France's "glorious revolution" but what actually became the French Revolution. It serves no

---

[6] An allegory – 'in which the apparent meaning of the characters and events us used to symbolise a deeper moral or spiritual meaning, or to illustrate truth or a moral.
[7] Thompson, Op. Cit.

purpose to rehearse the full facts here, nor is it clear that the centenary would have created any interest in Pentrich and South Wingfield. However, it certainly exercised the minds of upper and middle class radical thinkers.

The list of noted reformers cannot claim to be complete, there were others, some local, some national but they do follow a pattern in their activities. The main difference is probably their inclination to progress their views by their publications and speeches or by more positive action.

John Wilkes (1725-1797)

An English radical, journalist, politician and renowned philanderer, he was first elected Member of Parliament in 1757. He fought for the right of his voters, rather than the House of Commons, to determine their representatives. In 1768 angry protests by his supporters were suppressed in the St George's Fields Massacre. In 1771, he was instrumental in obliging the government to concede the right of printers to publish verbatim accounts of parliamentary debates. In 1776, he introduced the first Bill for parliamentary reform in the British Parliament. During the American War of Independence, he was a supporter of the American rebels, adding further to his popularity with American Whigs. In 1780, however, he commanded militia forces which helped put down the Gordon Riots against Catholic emancipation, damaging his popularity with many radicals. Many of Wilkes' followers saw this as a betrayal; some of them may have been among the rioters.

It is by no means certain that he featured in the readings of Thomas Bacon and it is doubtful they ever met. However, Wilkes did influence many of the radicals who did feature in Bacon's 'reading list'.

Thomas Paine (1737-1809)

Thomas Paine a Norfolk staymaker (female corsets) was perhaps an enduring influence on Bacon, possibly from the mid-1770's but far more likely during the period of the French Revolution, 1789-1799. Paine took a change in career in the early 1760's when he joined the Excise Service. He was dismissed twice, allegedly, for neglecting his duties; it may have been for his championing of excise officers' demands for more pay[8]. A change of surroundings offered itself when Paine managed to obtain letters of introduction from Benjamin Franklin, an American lawyer and future US Attorney General, who was studying law in London in the 1760's. Paine set off for the New World.

He embroiled himself in the American War of Independence, as a writer not a fighter, promoting the cause by his 1776 pamphlet *'Common Sense'* and his *'Crisis'* papers (1776-83). He was in favour of the American colonies struggle against George III and did much to keep American morale up during the war[9]. However, these papers were not widely distributed in England; they certainly would not have reached our man in Pentrich at this stage.

Green (1948) suggests that Paine was a powerful but unattractive figure; his private life was disreputable and sordid. Frequently drunk, filthy, quarrelsome, brutal to women he had seduced from their husband, he makes no claim on our sympathy'; and yet his *Rights of Man* was a masterly pamphlet[10].

Probably anticipating an unfriendly welcome in England he found himself in Paris in 1787, just before the French Revolution. He met and became close to one of the leaders, Condorcet[11]. Paine published his seminal work *'Rights of Man Pt.1'* (1791) concerned mainly with France and its constitution and in response to Edmund Burke's *'Reflections on the Revolution in France'*. He published *'Rights of Man Pt.2"*, concentrating on the follies of the so-called British Constitution in 1792[12].

---

[8] Royle, Edward. "Radical Politics 1790-1900 Religion and Belief" Longman (1971)
[9] Royle (1971) Op. Cit.
[10] Green, V.H.H. *"The Hanoverians"* pub Edward Arnold Ltd, London (1948)
[11] Marquis de Condorcet who took a leading role when the French Revolution swept France in 1789, hoping for a rationalist reconstruction of society, and championed many liberal causes.
[12] Royle (1971) Op. Cit. p.23

Although a religious man, he became an opponent of the Christian Church and his *'Age of Reason'* (1794) destroyed much of his credibility in America; he was already *persona non grata* in England.

His works, particularly *'The Rights of Man Pt.2'*, were well read in the various clubs and corresponding societies during the five or six years each side of 1800 and may have been considered a 'compulsory' text. If he had not read Paine's works before, Bacon would certainly have done during this period. However, it is undoubtedly true that Paine had a real influence on Bacon but we cannot be sure when this began. If I was to venture a time scale it would be around 1790/92 when Thomas was in his late thirties. There are several references to Bacon being an adherent of Paine and his views.

The Rights of Man was banned in 1794 but with so many in circulation this was probably a futile act on behalf of the government and, most likely, counterproductive.

There is no evidence or even a credible possibility that Thomas Bacon ever met Thomas Paine.

Edmund Burke (1729-1797)

Burke was a hugely influential Anglo-Irish politician, orator and political thinker, notable for his strong support for the American Revolution and, ironically, his fierce opposition to the French Revolution. Although he died when Bacon was 43, he may well have had some influence on his thinking, but, again, it is very unlikely they met.

Born in Dublin on 12 January 1729 the son of a solicitor, Burke was educated at Trinity College, Dublin and then went to London to study law. He quickly gave this up and after a visit to Europe settled in London, concentrating on a literary and political career. He became a member of parliament in 1765. He was closely involved in debates over limits to the power of the king, pressing for parliamentary control of royal patronage and expenditure.

Britain's imposition on America of measures including the Stamp Act in 1765 provoked violent colonial opposition. Burke argued that British policy had been inflexible and called for more pragmatism. He believed that government should be a cooperative relationship between rulers and subjects and that, while the past was important, a willingness to adapt to the inevitability of change could, hopefully, reaffirm traditional values under new circumstances. This would have been seen by many as the basis for radical thinking but, in Burke's view, a peaceful transition. However, Burke was no fan of consensus in dealing with the lower orders dismissing them as a 'swinish multitude'. In fact he was supported by the Bishop of London who could hardly believe 'the extreme depravity and licentiousness which prevails . . . amongst the lowest orders of the people. Didn't they know how lucky they were?

The outbreak of the French Revolution in 1789 gave Burke his greatest target. He expressed his hostility in *'Reflections on the Revolution in France'* (1790). The book provoked a huge response, including Thomas Paine's *'The Rights of Man'*. Burke emphasised the dangers of mob rule, fearing that the Revolution's fervour was destroying French society. He appealed to the British virtues of continuity, tradition, rank and property and opposed the Revolution to the end of his life.

Burke retired from parliament in 1794. His last years were clouded by the death of his only son, but he continued to write and defend himself from his critics. His arguments for long-lived constitutional conventions, political parties, and the independence of an MP once elected still carry weight. He is justly regarded as one of the founders of the British Conservative tradition. He died on 9 July 1797.

In reflecting on Burke's contribution to the debate it is worthwhile remembering that in the early years of the French Revolution the movement was largely monopolised by the 'men of rank and consequence' and not the working classes.

William Cobbett (1763-1835)

Whilst Bacon was undoubtedly influenced by Paine, in particular his *Rights of Man Pt 2*, it is debateable whether an even more significant direction was taken from William Cobbett who originally produced a weekly newspaper, the *Political Register* from 1802 originally promoting Tory views.

Interestingly, Cobbett had been publishing *Parliamentary Debates* as a supplement to his *Political Register*. In 1812 he sold this part of his business to his printer by the name of Thomas Curzon Hansard; the *Hansard* is still publishing Parliamentary debates to this day.

Cobbett soon moved to a more radical position, particularly in favour of widening (male) suffrage and parliamentary reform. Throughout 1815 and 1816 he was successful selling around 6,000 copies of each edition. His newspaper did not align itself with the views of the Government and they slapped a 4d stamp duty in 1815. These charges put his newspaper, at 6d or 7d a copy, beyond the means of other than the wealthy.

In 1816 Cobbett began publishing abstracts of the *Political Register* in pamphlet form at a cost of 2d. It quickly gained a circulation of 40,000. Critics dubbed it the *'Tuppeny Trash'*, a name Cobbett liked and made it the title. Forty thousand copies of the first issue were sold within a month. Henceforth the radical press aimed at a mass readership amongst the working classes[13].

Cobbett had been imprisoned in 1809 for seditious libel by criticising government use of German troops to deliver corporal punishment on British soldiers. After serving two years in Newgate he was in no mood to return. Rumours abounded of his imminent arrest for a second time promoted a swift departure to America in 1817 when *Habeas Corpus* was suspended. He left his publishing in the capable hands of William Benbow.

---

[13] Royle (1971) Op. Cit. p.28

When Cobbett returned to England in 1819 he brought back the remains of Thomas Paine who died earlier in the year.

It is known that Thomas Bacon read and promulgated the *Tuppeny Trash*, for example he gave John Cope a copy when attempting to gain access to Butterley Company arms and ironworks in May 1817.

Cobbett's *'Address to Journeymen and Labourers'* (October 1816), published in a two-penny, unstamped pamphlet designed for the widest possible circulation, also marked a new stage of the radical intellectual project in the plebeian public sphere, building on the critical insights into the new paper money system and its political economy developed in *"Paper Against Gold"*. Beginning with the 1816 address a complementary strategy of collective protest, co-ordinated through the radical press, was initiated for the political and economic liberation of the labouring classes, in Thompson's terminology *the working class*. These were the peak years of political activity in the working class public sphere, with the radical weekly occupying a central role in the wider radical / reformist movement.

Cobbett included a 'Letter to the Luddites' in the edition of the Political Register published in November 1816. He started his article by the paragraph 'It is undeniable, that you have committed acts of violence on the property of your neighbours, and have, in some instances, put themselves and their families in bodily fear. This is not to be denied, and it is deeply to be lamented....

After criticising the tactic of machine breaking he continued 'Your distress, that is to say, that which you now more immediately feel, arises from want of employment with wages sufficient for your support. The want of such employment has arisen from the want of a sufficient demand for the goods you make. The want of a sufficient demand for the goods you make has arisen from the want of means in the nation at large to purchase your goods. This want of means to purchase your goods has arisen from the weight of the taxes co-operating with the bubble of paper-money. The enormous burden of taxes and the bubble of paper-money have arisen from the war [against the French], the sinecures [support given to Anglican clergy], the standing army, the loans, and the stoppage of cash payments at the Bank; and it appears very clearly to me, that these never would have existed, if the Members of the House of Commons had been chosen annually by the people at large....

These are probably not quite the same form of words that those inclined to promote change through more 'direct action' would wish to hear but, nevertheless, they demonstrated sympathy for the radical's viewpoint. Along with William Horne's *Reformist Register* and the founding of Wooler's *Black Dwarf*[14], see below, a year later in 1817, this address by Cobbett signalled a new role for the unstamped weekly press as a vehicle for collective action. After long years of patient education of his public, Cobbett recognized that the time had now come for action, although not perhaps as far as insurrection: "Meeting after meeting, petition on petition, remonstrance on remonstrance, until the country be saved"[15]!

This was certainly a rallying call that would have resonated within Bacon's philosophy and his meetings.

However, White[16] suggests that Cobbett, with his shrewd sense of political possibilities, had uttered his warning against the dangers of the Club Movement from the beginning (The position of societies and clubs will be discussed in chapter 8). "I advise my countrymen to have nothing to do with any *Political Clubs*, any secret *Cabals,* any *Correspondencies,*" he wrote in *The Political Register*; but to trust to *individual exertions* and *open meetings*. He admitted that such clubs contained many worthy and zealous men, "but", he added, "I shall be very difficult to be made to believe that they are thus employing themselves in the best and most effectual way". However, it is known that he did, in fact, speak with respect of John Cartwright.

---

[14] Its title apparently alluded to the north-country belief in a malign magical fairy, responsible for all kinds of mischief—a notion that had been given contemporary form in Walter Scott's tale, 'The Black Dwarf', which appeared in his Tales of My Landlord in 1816.
[15] Cobbett, W. *"Political* Register 31 [16 Nov. 1816], 622
[16] White Op. Cit.

Cobbett's position on extreme radicalism is a little vague; he did talk of 'philosophical radicals'. He also expressed hatred of 'feelosafers', a group that may well have included Cartwright, Hunt and Burdett but certainly not Paine or Bacon.

Finally, it is known that Thomas Bacon would have heard Cobbett speak whilst at the Crown and Anchor meeting in January 1817, see chapter 10. However, there is no evidence or report they actually met or spoke.

Major John Cartwright (1740-1824)

John Cartwright, a political reformer, was descended from an old Nottinghamshire family. He was born on 17 September 1740 and was educated at the grammar school in Newark and at a private academy in Heath, Yorkshire. At about the age of eighteen he entered the navy and saw some active service under the command of Lord Howe. Whilst serving he did save men from drowning on at least two occasions.

Cartwright became seriously ill and in 1770 he returned to England to convalesce. He took a keen interest in politics and in 1774 Cartwright published *American Independence: the Glory and Interest of Great Britain*. Cartwright criticised British foreign policy and argued that the American people had the right to choose their own rulers and to tax themselves and advocated "a political union based upon a commonwealth of interest". The pamphlet upset the authorities and brought an end to his naval career. Instead, he was appointed as a major in the Nottinghamshire militia, which led to his being called Major Cartwright for the rest of his life.

In about 1775 Cartwright publicly began to assert his opinions on political matters in '*A Letter to Edmund Burke*', controverting the Principles of American Government laid down in his lately published speech on American Taxation, and in a tract on American independence. Two years later his sympathies hindered him from joining Lord Howe's command in North America, and a stop was thus put to his professional advancement.

In 1775 Cartwright began a series of writings on reform in parliament: his most famous pamphlet was '*Take your Choice*' (1776). From the first he advocated reforms such as annual parliaments, universal suffrage, and secret ballots. His extreme notions hindered his acceptance by the Whigs, but his position as a country gentleman ensured him respect. He was frequently in correspondence with Edmund Burke and other leaders of opinion. In 1780 Cartwright began the agitation which earned for him the title of the Father of Reform. A county meeting in Nottingham was succeeded in March of that year by the historic meeting at Westminster, on which occasion the leaders of the Whig opposition met Cartwright and his friends, and passed resolutions on the inadequate representation of the people of England. Shortly afterwards, he founded the Society for Constitutional Information. He stood for parliament on a number of occasions: he contested Nottinghamshire in 1780 and Boston in 1806 and 1807, and was nominated for Westminster in 1818 and 1819. He was unsuccessful on every occasion.

Meanwhile he was actively engaged in agricultural pursuits and laying down practical hints for the encouragement of the farming interest. He was likewise in active co-operation with Clarkson, Granville Sharp, and the other anti-slavery leaders. During the alarmist period of the early 1790's Cartwright ran personal risk. Having attended a public meeting to celebrate the taking of the Bastille, his promotion in the militia was withheld, and his commission at length cancelled.

He contributed many papers to Cobbett's Register and he continued to publish numerous writings, of which the more important were: The Comparison: in which Mock Reform, Half Reform, and Constitutional Reform are considered; or, who are the Statesmen to preserve our Laws and Liberties (1810); Six Letters to the Marquis of Tavistock, on a Reform of the Commons House of Parliament (1812); The English Constitution produced and illustrated (1823).

In 1813 he was arrested in the course of a political tour, but soon released; and in 1820 was tried for sedition and fined £100.

In 1805 Cartwright left his Lincolnshire home and went to London, residing for some time at Enfield. In 1810 he removed to James Street, Buckingham Gate, and in 1819 to Burton Crescent, where he resided till his death on 23 September 1824.

The end of the Napoleonic War and the economic depression which accompanied it produced a revival of political activity from Major Cartwright. Hampden Clubs, sometimes called the Friends of Parliamentary Reform" and societies for political reform were founded by him as he toured the country[17]. He then toured the country encouraging other parliamentary reformers to follow his example. Cartwright's main objective was to unite middle class moderates with radical members of the working class. This worried the authorities and led to Cartwright's arrest and detention for a short while in Huddersfield in 1813.

Although Cartwright, together with others such as Cobbett and Hunt, struggled to direct the energies of followers into political channels he was not always successful. The clubs were regarded with suspicion by the authorities, which saw them as breeding grounds for the growing radicalism of the times. On 9 February 1817 a secret Parliamentary Committee report concluded that the real object of the Hampden Clubs and similar institutions was to foment "an insurrection, so formidable from numbers, as by dint of physical strength to overpower all resistance".

The government began to introduce legislation, such as the Seditious Meetings Act, and it became more difficult for political clubs to meet. For example, the Birmingham Hampden Club, founded in September 1816 and boasting 300 regular attendees by the following January, had a moderate ethos and publicly condemned violence after a local riot, but struggled to find venues as publicans were pressured not to permit club meetings on their premises. Private rooms were found, but by April 1817, in an atmosphere of suspicion and with the government spy and *agent provocateur* William Oliver, also known as W.T. Richards, active in the city, regular club meetings were suspended. In Manchester the movement's

---

[17] Bamford, S *"Early Days and Passages in the Life of A Radical"* ed. H. Dunckley, T. Fisher Unwin 893)

leaders were targeted by the city's deputy constable, Joseph Nadin, who arrested many of them, including Samuel Bamford, after the unrest of March 1817 and sent them to London in irons, where some spent months in prison before their release without charge. With the Hampden clubs stifled, the Lancashire leadership formed the Patriotic Union Society, and it was this body that called the 1819 public meeting for political reform that became the Peterloo Massacre.

Although they shared the same name, the Hampden Clubs formed in Pentrich, Ripley and elsewhere by Bacon and his friends were very different from the middle class 'talking shops' created by Cartwright.

Thompson[18] gave a succinct quote on the relevance of Cartwright; "Major Cartwright defined as early as this the main claims he never swerved. Incapable of compromise, eccentric and courageous, the Major pursued his single-minded course, issuing letters, appeals, and pamphlets, from his seat in Boston, Lincolnshire, surviving trials, tumults, dissension and repression."

As we outline in the next chapter, Bacon would certainly have been in Cartwright's presence and heard him speak, if not quite a close friend.

Sir Francis Burdett (1770-1844)

Burdett was the most prominent radical member of the House of Commons and had been seeking both parliamentary and economic reform for some time. As early as May 1797 he had chaired a meeting, organised by John Cartwright, at the Crown and Anchor tavern calling for reform[19]. There were as many as 1,100 to 1,200 diners.

It was suggested to the Pentrich Revolutionaries that Burdett was waiting in the wings to take over as the leader, or even President, of the 'Republic'.

---

[18] Thompson, Op. Cit.
[19] Gault, op. cit.

It is probable that Burdett knew little if anything about Thomas Bacon and Pentrich men before their arrest and conviction.

William Benbow (1784-1841)

William Benbow was born in Manchester in 1784. As a young man he became a Nonconformist preacher, most likely a Quaker, with radical political opinions. A shoemaker, Benbow became one of the leaders of the reform movement in Manchester.

Benbow attended political meetings in London during 1816 as a delegate of one of the Lancashire Hampden Clubs, and became interested in Spenceanism. He was closely involved with planning the attempted Blanketeers protest march by Lancashire weavers in March 1817 and was one of a number of radicals arrested in the wake of this event and the subsequent severe crackdown by the authorities, amidst rumours that mass uprisings were being plotted in industrial centres like Manchester. His protest petition to Parliament in 1818, presented along with a number of others, describes how he was apprehended in Dublin on 16 May 1817, spent eight months on remand in London then was released without trial, lacking the resources to travel home to Manchester. He established himself as a political radical in London, where he was an associate of William Cobbett and passed his time "agitating the labouring classes at their trades meetings and club-houses" according to the memoirs of the Manchester radical Samuel Bamford, who also spent several months in the Coldbath Fields Prison in London and petitioned Parliament unsuccessfully for redress.

To support himself and his radical activities Benbow worked as a printer, publisher and bookseller, and also as a coffee house proprietor. In addition to political texts, he also produced pirated editions of other works, and pornography - around 1818 he employed the young William Dugdale who went on to become one of London's most notorious publishers of obscene and pornographic material. He was closely linked to the writer and publisher George Cannon, printing and marketing a number of his works and translations, and it has been suggested that some of the writings published under Benbow's name may have been written by Cannon. When William Cobbett fled to America in 1817 to avoid arrest, his radical newspaper, the Political Register, continued to be published in London by Benbow until his return in 1820.

With Benbow's Manchester connections and Bacon's frequent visit to Manchester it is possible they would have met.

Samuel Bamford (1788-1872)

Bamford was what to-day might be called a 'portfolio' worker; he was a teacher, handloom weaver, radical, poet and composer of religious songs – brought up a staunch Methodist. He was born in Middleton, Manchester in 1788.

Like Thomas Bacon he was influenced by radicals such as Thomas Paine, William Cobbett and later by Major John Cartwright. He attended the key meetings at the Crown and Anchor as a northerner delegate and Hampden Reform Club member. He knew Bacon well and they would have travelled together on occasions. He was arrested in March 1817 on a charge of treason. At his trial in London he was acquitted due to insufficient evidence. He was, perhaps, more of an academic radical than Bacon. His autobiography *"Passage in the Life of a Radical"* contains an important account of the Peterloo Massacre, which he witnessed, and references to his meetings with Thomas Bacon, Oliver the Spy and Brandreth[20].

Thomas Wooler (1786-1853)

The publisher Thomas Jonathan Wooler was active in the Radical movement of early 19th century Britain, best known for his satirical journal *'The Black Dwarf'*. This was a satirical weekly radical journal. It started in January 1817 in response to the government crackdowns of that month and

---

[20] Autobiography of Samuel Bamford (1788-1872), 'The Middleton Poet', edited by Henry Dunckley, published by T. Unwin Fisher, London, 1893 – see chapter XXIII

pursued a strong editorial line of parliamentary reform. Within three months, Wooler was arrested and charged with seditious libel, but was found not guilty.

In its heyday the paper sold around 12,000 copies every week and had a strong following among working people. This was despite its cover price of 4d (about half a day's wages for a craftsman, or the cost of eight pints of beer).

He was born in Yorkshire and lived there for a short time before moving to London as a printer's apprentice. He worked for the radical journal *The Reasoner*, and then became editor of *The Statesman*. His interest in legal matters led him to write and publish the pamphlet *An Appeal to the Citizens of London against the Packing of Special Juries* in 1817.

In response to the Gagging Acts (Treason Act 1817 and Seditious Meetings Act 1817) passed by the British government in January 1817, Wooler started publishing '*The Black Dwarf*' as a new radical unstamped (untaxed) journal. Within three months, he was arrested and charged with seditious libel. The prosecution claimed that Wooler had written articles libelling Lord Liverpool's government, but Wooler, defending himself, convinced the jury that, although he had published the article, he had not written it himself, and therefore was not guilty. He continued to publish '*The Black Dwarf*' and to use it to argue for parliamentary reform.

Wooler was an active supporter of Major John Cartwright and his Hampden Club movement.

Gravener Henson (1785-1852)

It is by no means certain that Bacon was influenced by Henson but there is a strong possibility in view of the latter's involvement in radical activities in Nottingham. He was born in 1785 in humble circumstances, his education was scanty, but he managed to gather an accurate knowledge of the commercial laws of England. He was active in seeking to reform the

Combination Acts of 1799 and 1800 and, in particular, the bias in prosecution of misdemeanours of the employees compared with those by employers.

According to Stevens[21], he was the leader of the Nottingham hosiery and lace workers who had tried unsuccessfully to promote a bill in 1812 to protect them against various abuses of the trade. Although a newspaper accused him of being implicit in the Pentrich business, he was able to contradict the report since he was arrested in London on 11th April 1817 on suspicion, and held in jail without trial until the following November. Furthermore the government suspected Henson of helping to plot the Pentrich Rising and this maybe explains his arrest and detention without trial under the suspension of Habeas Corpus.

On the day of his arrest, the Home Office sent a special messenger to Nottingham asking the authorities to search Henson's home before his friends got to hear of his detention[22]. The authorities were after Luddite papers which a prisoner under sentence at Leicester had said might be found at Henson's house. A search was made on 12th April but nothing was found. Despite the disappearance of the Luddite papers, if any, the Home Office paper listed Henson as 'one of the Principal Persons by whose Agency the Pentrich Conspiracy was set on foot and carried on, besides the unhappy Men who were convicted at Derby . . .' The Home Office believed he was behind plans to attack arms depots and barracks, including Weedon. It would seem that Henson was an enigma and the part he played in the various incidents was never clearly established. However, it is certainly true that Henson knew the greater part of the Luddite story, if indeed, he did not organise it.

In his seminal work *"The Making of the English Working Class"*, Thompson[23] offers the opinion that Gravener Henson was one of the few truly impressive trade union leaders who emerged in these early years. Henson exemplifies the struggle of the outworkers, touching the fringes of

---

[21] Stevens, John (1977) Op. Cit.
[22] HO/79/3 quoted in Stevens (1977) Op. Cit.
[23] Thompson, (1980) Op. Cit.

Luddism, organising their illegal union, sharing their advanced political Radicalism, and attempting until 1824 to enforce or enact protective legislation in their favour. He died in poverty in 1852.

There is direct evidence that Bacon was influenced by these men, other than perhaps, Paine, Cobbett and Cartwright, but they were the source of key documents supporting a reform agenda. It should be added that the feelings of these men, although strongly held, were that they should be pursued by peaceful persuasion, the presentation of petitions and the power of speech.

Thomas Spence (1750-1814)

Spence was one of the leading English revolutionaries of the late eighteenth and early nineteenth centuries. Spence was born in poverty and died the same way in 1814 after long periods of imprisonment.

At the centre of Spence's work was his Plan, known as 'Spence's Plan'. The Plan has a number of features, including:
1. The end of aristocracy and landlords;
2. All land should be publicly owned by 'democratic parishes', which should be largely self-governing;
3. Rents of land in parishes to be shared equally amongst parishioners;
4. Universal suffrage (including female suffrage) at both parish level and through a system of deputies elected by parishes to a national senate;
5. A 'social guarantee' extended to provide income for those unable to work;
6. The 'rights of infants' to be free from abuse and poverty.

Spence's Plan was first published in his penny pamphlet *Property in Land Every One's Right* in 1775. It was re-issued as *The Real Rights of Man* in later editions. It was also reissued by, amongst others, Henry Hyndman under the title of *The Nationalization of the Land in 1795 and 1882*.

Spence may have been the first Englishman to speak of 'the rights of man'. The following recollection, composed in the third person, was written by Spence while he was in prison in London in 1794 on a charge of High Treason. Spence was, he wrote,

> *the first, who as far as he knows, made use of the phrase "RIGHTS OF MAN", which was on the following remarkable occasion: A man who had been a farmer, and also a miner, and who had been ill-used by his landlords, dug a cave for himself by the seaside, at Marsdon Rocks, between Shields and Sunderland, about the year 1780, and the singularity of such a habitation, exciting the curiosity of many to pay him a visit; our author was one of that number. Exulting in the idea of a human being, who had bravely emancipated himself from the iron fangs of aristocracy, to live free from impost, he wrote extempore with chaulk above the fire place of this free man, the following lines:*
> *Ye landlords vile, whose man's peace mar,*
> *Come levy rents here if you can;*
> *Your stewards and lawyers I defy,*
> *And live with all the RIGHTS OF MAN*

Spence left Newcastle for London in 1787. He kept a book-stall in High Holborn. In 1794 he spent seven months in Newgate Gaol on a charge of High Treason, and in 1801 he was sentenced to twelve months' imprisonment for seditious libel. He died in London on 8 September 1814.

The Society of Spencean Philanthropists (including Arthur Thistlewood) was involved in the Cato Street Conspiracy of 1820.

5. Radicalising Tommy

In tying together his upbringing and early years, there must have been a specific period in Thomas Bacon's life when he first developed his awareness that society was not fair and that people of his social class were not treated well. Furthermore, there must then have been a second stage when he decided to do something about, or at the very least, to seek out people of a like mind. It seems that the time when the French Revolution was becoming common knowledge, around 1790, was a period when some of the working class grew aware of wider events, became politically active and some also recognised that the agenda of the working class was substantially different to that of their employers and the ruling elite.

There had, of course, been several middle class radicals demanding a peaceful transition to parliamentary reform for many years; indeed some are mentioned in the previous chapter. Looking back it seems that once the movement encompassed the working class there were moves to take a more direct approach over the next forty or so years. It is arguably a crucial stage when the lower orders became aware of the Americans achieving a republic and the French, whilst it is admitted not predominantly the lower orders, removing their King and taking an element of control.

It is known that Thomas Bacon became an adherent of Thomas Paine probably as a result of his *"Rights of Man Part 2"* which began to be circulated around England in 1792-93. This second part in Paine's series is more inclined to the situation in England than in America or France and it was written as a challenge to Burke's *"Reflections on the French Revolution"*.

In seeking out evidence of when Thomas Bacon's radical feelings emerged one can only highlight incidents, events or situations he may have been aware of. As mentioned previously, he would certainly have observed the wealthy trundling along the Birmingham / Sheffield turnpike which passed close to Pentrich at Buckland Hollow. He would doubtless have experienced the harsh treatment handed out to some weavers in the village by the master weaver's agents; but this was life! He would have seen the impact of the Enclosures in removing traditional growing or grazing land from working families. He would also be aware of the dramatic changes in the price and availability of basic foodstuffs.

At some stage in his late teens he would be accepted into the male domain of the White Horse Public House in the village especially as it was run by his widowed sister Nancy. He would find copies of newspapers and pamphlets left in the pub and being literate he would be able read them – maybe being required to read them to other customers less skilled in the art.

As we have indicated, he may also have visited the local inns along the turnpike route, which was in walking distance from his home, such as the *Cock Inn, Ripley, Devonshire Arms, Buckland Hollow, The Anchor* and the *Peacock, Oakerthorpe*. These are the places he would find travellers well versed in the changes underway across the land and willing to talk of their experiences. Of course, like any fable or traveller's tales they were 'enhanced' with the telling and re-telling.

As suggested in previous chapters, Tommy would have been given a Christian up-bringing and his reading would have started with the Bible. However, other books may have been around, for example many young men would have read Bunyan's *Pilgrim's Progress* and, seeing through the allegory, maybe dreamt of a life beyond their current situation.

Thomas was a tall, well-built young man, his sharp brain and ability to read and write would have given him some status in the community. He may well have been looked towards for guidance in difficult times. Looking back from the reports of meetings held in 1815-1817 it was evident that Thomas Bacon was clearly accepted as a leading light in the area and even beyond. It is quite remarkable to imagine Bacon addressing an audience containing men who had gained the benefit of a 'proper' education at a grammar school or even university. He must have worked hard to temper his Derbyshire accent in order to be understood and to develop the confidence for public speaking.

Even in small places like Pentrich, industrial changes were slowly having an impact. In 1785 Arkwright patents run out and technology became widely available. This period saw an increase in the spread of factories and the realisation that more could be produced by using many machines in one location and, at the same time, by using less of the well-paid skilled men.

Around this time, and for the first time in history, children became important factors in the economic system[24]. Bacon, age 31 in 1785, would doubtless see indications that children of the village were beginning to be used in organised employment rather than helping at home.

As Bacon was aware of Paine's writing, '*Rights of Man Pt.2*', it will be interesting to reproduce one paragraph published in 1792 when Thomas Bacon was 37 that may have been an inspiration. A short phrase from the preface to demonstrate Paine's complex argument:

> *I do not believe that the people of England have ever been fairly and candidly dealt by. They have been imposed upon by parties, and by men assuming the character of leaders. It is time that the nation should rise above those trifles. It is time to dismiss that inattention which has so long been the encouraging cause of stretching taxation to excess. It is time to dismiss all those songs and toasts which are calculated to enslave, and operate to suffocate reflection. On all such subjects men have but to think, and they will neither act wrong nor be misled. To say that any people are not fit for freedom, is to make poverty their choice, and to say they had rather be loaded with taxes than not. If such a case could be proved, it would equally prove that those who govern are not fit to govern them, for they are a part of the same national mass.*[25]

These are certainly powerful words and whilst not a direct call to arms not, at least, in the first instance, one can imagine how it may have been read and where the emphasis could be made by those with a more direct agenda.

---

[24] Royston Pike, E. *"Human Documents of the Industrial Revolution"* George Allen & Unwin Ltd (1966) p. 75
[25] Paine, Thomas (1792) *"Rights of Man Part 2"* a paragraph from the preface.

It takes very little imagination to see Thomas reading this to a group of men in the White Horse who, with the clarity of rough ale, would see that it referred to them and to their situation!

It is known that his father died in 1797 when Thomas would have been 43; as a single man he may have been caring for his elderly father, he was living in the same house in Pentrich.

However, we can only assume that between the years between the beginning of the French Revolution, his introduction to Paine's ideas, between 1792-93 and his suspected appearance as a Luddite leader around 1810, he be would expanding his contacts, reinforcing his knowledge and solidifying his radical credentials.

The employment prospects for the stockinger were variable, the years around 1795 saw many food riots around the country; life was not easy. However, in the area around Pentrich and Ripley, employment prospects must have been enhanced by the opening of Butterley Company foundry after 1790 and more of the factories and mines.

There were various 'secret societies' of radicals around the East Midlands, based mainly in Nottingham, Leicester and Derby. As a budding radical, Bacon would doubtless need to have spent a period of time developing his credibility, reliability and becoming accepted as a trusted colleague in an arena wider than just Pentrich, South Wingfield and surrounding villages. Those involved in the radical movements, the beginning of Luddite groups, would have been aware of spies and informers; new-comers would not be accepted easily. The close-knit nature of the villages would, of course, mean that everyone's background was general knowledge.

As far as current research can establish and during this period immediately prior to the detailed planning for the Pentrich Rising, there is no evidence that Thomas Bacon ever met Jeremiah Brandreth. It is known, however, that Brandreth was an active Luddite in the Nottingham area. It seems unlikely that he did not, at least, know of his existence; probably well before he was introduced as the replacement leader in June 1817.

Bacon was suspected of Luddite activities in 1810 to 1814 and it seems he would have been a favourite to lead the direct action against what they would see as exploitation of the workers. However, it should be remembered that at the time of the Luddite activity in Pentrich, Swanwick and South Wingfield, Thomas was in his late 50's. One would have imagined that frame breaking and the associated violence was a sport for the younger man.

After the Luddite period, it is clear that Bacon embarked on a succession of meetings, planning sessions and organising activities to take his radical views to a significantly higher level. It was at this point that he increased his travel around England. It is not clear whether he took on the role of the 'Derbyshire Delegate' voluntarily or was persuaded to do so.

At some point he seemed to move from a localised agenda typified by protesting and direct action against poverty, industrialisation, oppressive employers and frame masters to something quite different. The step up, if that is what it was, would be to work towards parliamentary reform, demanding such changes as annual parliaments, universal male suffrage and secret elections – the reformist's agenda. What is not clear is the point at which Thomas Bacon saw insurrection and the creation of a republic as his favoured option – maybe it always was!

Furthermore, it seems that Thomas subscribed to achieving these aims by radicalising the movement and not the softer ways of many middle-class reformers who preferred words, pamphlets and petitions rather than direct action; Cobbett's 'feelosafers'.

It is established that Bacon was prompting William Cobbett's *'Tuppenny Trash'* to John Cope, a Butterley Company employee and potential revolutionary in May 1817. The short version of Cobbett's *'Register'*, originally published in 1812, began in 1816 when Bacon would have been 62. Another of Cobbett's works Bacon read to others was the *'Address to Journeymen and Labourers'* also published in 1816.

Major Cartwright was a national figure with a Nottinghamshire base and was known to Bacon. As a 'delegate' to the various radical meetings in the North, it is almost certain that Bacon would also have met William Benbow.

As with the publications of Paine and Cobbett, Bacon would have read and probably distributed copies of Wooler's *'Black Dwarf'*.

Thomas Bacon was at several points during the trial given the title the 'Nestor of the Pentrich Revolutionaries'. Nestor was a hero celebrated as an elderly and wise counsellor to the Greeks at Troy; a venerable and wise old man. I am sure he would have enjoyed this status. He was even wise enough to ensure that he kept his head when many about him were losing theirs!

Bacon was an active supporter of the *Doctrines of Liberty and Equality* and a zealous disciple of Thomas Paine. He believed property should be equalised, the landed estate broken up and eight acres distributed to each man. For Bacon, Cobbett's *"Register"* and the Hampden Clubs did not go far enough. Whilst he claimed to be seeking the basic aims such as male suffrage and annual parliaments, he was known to have called for the break-up of great estates and the allocation of a few acres to each man[26].

A Three-Cornered Hat

Although it is a natural human reaction to 'pigeon-hole' people from a political perspective. For example, socialists, republicans, liberals, conservatives and so on, it does not reveal a true, or indeed, complete picture. In to-day's political language we see hues of red, blue, green and yellow but in the period of Thomas Bacon's life there were always many different shades of grey. Many of the political positions were based even more on class than they are to-day. It seems to me that in Bacon's time there were three variants of radical although the boundaries between them were not watertight.

---

[26] Thompson, Op. Cit.

We have the 'reformer', typified by Cobbett and 'Orator' Hunt, seeking parliamentary reform, universal suffrage (for the male population at this stage) and secret ballots. They pursued their aims by power of speech, erudite argument and petitions. As to-day, opinions varied, for example, some saw Henry Hunt as an effective orator for the reformist agenda, whilst others thought him a garrulous windbag who liked the sound of his own voice.

We have the politically motivated radical seeking reform by more direct or extreme means, maybe even carrying a 'republican' banner. In the context of Bacon's time, the foremost might be Thomas Burke. I would place Thomas Bacon, the elder Ludlam, Turner and Jeremiah Brandreth in this group.

Finally, we have the largest group of the lot, the local disgruntled working class family man, often demonstrating against more mundane issues such as poverty, low wages, industrialisation, oppressive employers, lack of food, amongst many grievances. The foot soldiers of the Blanketeers and the Pentrich Rising would be typical of this group. It should not be forgotten that most would have no truck with insurrection; they wanted a better life, a peaceful life and enough food for their families to eat. These would be the people, who after the initial burst of excitement or local pressure, chose to drift away and were later to deny any involvement in the Rising.

In his paper on Bacon[27], Prof Malcolm Thomis sees him as a professional revolutionary, a veteran Jacobin since the time of Paine whereas the other local principles, such as Turner, Ludlam and Weightman, as 'amateur revolutionaries.

The Impact of Religion

It has long been accepted that, for those who could read, Bunyan's *Pilgrim's Progress* and Pain's *Rights of Man Pt.2* were the standard texts

---

[27] Thomis, Malcolm *"The Guilt of Thomas Bacon of Pentrich"* The Derbyshire Archaeological Journal

of the late eighteenth century radical – much more so than the Bible. Whilst there is no direct evidence of Thomas Bacon reading the first publication, he certainly was influenced by the second. It was a time when working people were beginning to see themselves as a section of society with different interest and needs than those of their 'betters' – the ruling and employing classes.

The French Revolution from 1789 was, to a great extent, the instigator of what was named the Jacobin agitation of the 1790's. Many contemporary writers supported the Revolution, including Coleridge and Wordsworth, that was until the Reign of Terror and the obvious thirst for blood revised their position somewhat.

Whilst space precludes a thorough discussion of the impact of religion, the established Church was losing much of its power with regard to the working class. The conservative approach, close association with the ruling classes, the massive church estates, compulsory tithes, the hierarchy of the clergy and the regularly preached mantra of being satisfied with your station in life and not seeking or even contemplating any improvement; all served to the faithful to consider their position.

Dissent against the stories of the Bible caused many not to challenge God but to disassociate themselves from the rigidity of the miracles and associated text. In cannot have helped when many of the clergy were the second or third son of the landed gentry

The Methodist movement, formed by John Wesley in the 1730's seemed to be focusing on the average person and seeking to help the poor. John Wesley always declared that his movement should remain within the Anglican Church but the Church of England was keen to distance itself from him and his followers. However, the Methodist Church grew mainly amongst the poor and in many urban and rural areas of Britain. In the end, the strength and impact of Methodism made a separate Methodist Church inevitable. In 1795, four years after Wesley's death, Methodists in Britain became legally able to conduct marriages and perform the sacraments.

Many Methodist preachers were closer to the working people forming their congregations and, as such, were often seem as supporting, if not quite promoting, the radical movement. For example, in Huddersfield the church was labelled 'Tom Paine's Methodists'.

During the period from 1816 to 1817 and, perhaps onwards, Primitive Methodism took great hold amongst the working class in central Derbyshire. It should not be forgotten that Isaac Ludlam, one of the three who were hanged and beheaded, was a well-respected Methodist lay preacher.

6. Visiting America

One of the challenges in plotting the life of Thomas Bacon surrounds the tentative claims that he was both a war veteran and that he visited America at least once. Neal informs us that Thomas Bacon visited 'once if not twice in America'. The original texts give no clues as to when he may have made such a journey and where and in which war he may have served. I feel unable to repeat these assertions without due consideration.

It is interesting to explore the opportunities for these claims and the evidence to support the statements, as far as is possible. They could, of course, both be genuine and also been achieved concurrently.

Although it is not conclusive, using the precise word 'visited' is an indication that Bacon was not serving under the King's colours at the time he was alleged to have visited America, one can explore the possibility of a social visit – but to what end? He may have travelled as a fare-paying passenger on one of the many ships sailing across the Atlantic. Many thousands travelled to America between 1700 and up to the start of the War of Independence in 1775, many were slaves but it is thought over 210,000 Europeans made the journey with a view to settlement, in fact it was being encouraged. The movement began again in earnest after 1783.

In particular, prior to the war the British government were keen to transport Europeans to populate their 'new empire' whilst not reducing the labour force back home too much. Many Germans, Scandinavians and Dutch made this journey and formed colonies in America. In fact the cost was reduced by half between 1720 and 1770 to increase the flow, by this latter date Thomas would have been 16. An unlikely scenario!

Understandably, travel by potential settlers and traders reduced considerably during the years of the war.

A search for an alternative theory to explain Bacon's supposed visit to America would be as a soldier during the War of Independence when Thomas would be 21 to 29, certainly the ages are feasible. This would serve to remove the testing question of how he came by the funds for the journey.

If he did join the British army was it voluntarily or was he 'pressed' into service? Press gangs were not uncommon but operated primarily to gather men for the Navy and, in addition, usually took merchant seamen with some relevant experience at sea or on rivers. There is no evidence that Bacon possessed either of these qualifications. Moving inland and pressing men from non-maritime trades was highly unusual.

The use of impressment for the Army was not as common as it was for the navy but it was used for a short time during this period. Whilst engaged in the American Revolutionary War, after the losses at the Battle of Saratoga and the apprehended hostilities with France, the existing voluntary enlistment measures were judged to be insufficient. Between 1775 and 1781, the regular army increased from 48,000 to 110,000, many regular troops were sent from Ireland.

Two acts were passed, the Recruiting Act 1778 and the Recruiting Act 1779, for the impression of individuals into the British Army. The Recruiting Act of 1779 was repealed on 26 May 1780, and army impressment was permanently discontinued.

During the experiment, the British government allowed army impressment under severely restricted circumstances, both acts emphasized volunteering over impressment and offered strong incentives for men to volunteer. The impressment portion of the 1778 Act applied only to Scotland and the area around London, excluding Wales and the rest of England, to avoid interfering with harvesting and other essential work. The 1779 Act applied to all of Great Britain, but was initially suspended everywhere except the area around London, and actually applied to all of Great Britain for only six months, until the 1779 act was repealed in May 1780, and army impressment ceased in Britain.

This would seem to cast significant doubt on army press gangs ever finding their way to Pentrich in central Derbyshire. There would have been richer pickings in the more heavily populated areas.

Unlike naval impressment, army impressment applied only to "able-bodied" men and not, what were legally termed, 'idle and disorderly persons' such as vagrants, petty thieves, smugglers, etc. It also excluded men who could, upon reasonable examination, prove themselves to exercise and industriously follow some lawful trade or employment, or to have some substance sufficient for their support and maintenance. The 1778 law excluded any men who were voters, or harvest workers. The 1779 law did extend impressment to 'incorrigible rogues' who had abandoned their families, and left them as expenses on the parish. Impressed apprentices were released under appeal from their masters and impressed foreigners were released when requested by their countries' embassies.[28]

There would appear to be little substance to support the theory that Bacon visited America as a soldier. In addition, there were no army regiments recruiting specifically in Derbyshire until Victorian times.

Creating a simple chronology for a private visit to America provides a narrow window before the American War of Independence, by which time Bacon was only 22 or 23. The conclusion that I am seeking to substantiate suggests that Bacon became a serious radical around 1792 around the age of 37. Being devoid of any reasonable evidence, I must conclude that Bacon did not in fact visit America during this short period.

If the claims that Thomas Bacon was involved in Luddite activities from 1810 to 1812 or a little later and there are many references to this, it leaves a second possible window between 1784 and 1809. He would have been 30 years of age at the start of this period and 55 at the end; this would potentially leave sufficient time. One would imagine that the round trip to America and return would take several months, probably a year. This does

---

[28] Curtis, Edward, "The Organization of the British Army in the American Revolution." 1972, ISBN 0-85409-906-9

not of course give any clue as to where he obtained the funds and, of course, there is no definitive evidence to support this proposal.

A final brief window of opportunity is revealed between the end of his Luddite activities and the well documented series of meeting associated with his radical activities and the preparation for the Rising, roughly 1812 to 1816. This stage would have covered his age from 58 to 62. Other sources provide evidence that Thomas Bacon was deeply engaged in his 'radical' activities in this period.

Whilst lacking any evidence at this stage, if he did visit America, it was potentially most likely between 1784 and 1809.

The transatlantic crossing, in this pre-steam era, would take six to twelve weeks depending on weather, time spent waiting in port for an economic cargo, the route taken and many other delaying issues.

The cost was difficult to ascertain with some precision. It would seem that the actual cost was, to some extent, at the whim of vessel's captain or owner. It has been estimated that it would cost around ⅓ of a labourer's wage. In 1800 a labourer in England would earn around 11 shillings or 55p a week, around £28.60 per year, assuming he had work all year round which was by no means a certainty. The single fare could be as much as £9.50. It is clear that Bacon did not have the support of an affluent family.

He could have 'worked his passage' as a crew member but this appears highly unlikely. He was brought up as far from the sea in England as one can get in England and one cannot imagine any captain paying unskilled seamen.

Therefore, without factoring in the travel to Liverpool and general living expenses, where would Tommy Bacon get £20? It is recorded that he financed his trips around England primarily by collecting pennies from local supporters. There is no record of Bacon enjoying the patronage of any well-heeled member of the middle or higher classes. In fact, his reputation in Derbyshire would seem to indicate that no-one with the necessary finances would wish to sponsor Thomas Bacon.

What other evidence do we have, compelling or otherwise? We know that Thomas was greatly influenced by Thomas Paine and that Paine was in America from 1774 to 1787 and it was there that he first published his radical paper 'Common Sense'. However, this was a pamphlet not widely circulated in Britain.

Paine had arrived in America with a letter of introduction from Benjamin Franklin (later to be the American Attorney General), who was studying law in London. It is inconceivable that Thomas Bacon moved in these circles, particularly if he was a common solider.

One cannot categorically state that Thomas Bacon was not a solider but it seems an extremely unlikely scenario. From the character we are building of Thomas bacon, serving as one of the King's soldiers does not ring true!

We need to approach this topic within the context of the late eighteenth and early nineteenth centuries. Any travel by the working classes was problematic and, in most cases, totally alien. Matters did change later with more factories, growing towns and cities, better roads and, eventually, railways – but not yet!

On the balance of probabilities, it seems highly unlikely Thomas Bacon visited America either as a soldier or as a private traveller. Moreover there is no evidence he served as a soldier anywhere.

Finally on this point, Bacon was obviously concerned about his image and in developing his standing within the radical community. To suggest that he had been to America may well have been useful in bolstering his status as a republican. If Bacon was a strong republican, as to evidence seems to indicate, the questions arises to why, if he did in fact visit the land of the opportunity, why he came back to Pentrich?

7. Luddites and the Rest

Riots, protests and relatively small-scale disturbances were a common feature of the British life throughout the eighteenth century, particularly in the rapidly developing towns. The causes were many and varied from on-going grievances to specific incidents. It is true to say that the disturbances were far more likely to be connected with the price or shortages of food, raw materials or localised employment issues rather than the radical/reformist agenda.

For example, high cheese prices resulted in the 'Great Cheese Riots' at Nottingham. The whole affair was exaggerated by the fact that the riots coincided with the City's Goose Fair of early October 1776 when the streets were crowded and many were 'under the influence' of some strong midlands beverage. It is alleged that the mayor was knocked over by a stolen cheese rolling down a Nottingham street, doubtless a very serious matter. At a more severe level, periodic food riots continued in many towns well into the nineteenth century.

In the industrial context short-lived strikes and more serious incidents such as frame-breaking, although localised, were quite common.

A prototype of James Hargreaves 'Spinning Jenny' was destroyed following fears that the invention could impact on men's livelihoods; which of course, together with other inventions, it did! Sporadic incidents of frame-breaking and food riots took place over many years. Porter (1982)[29] emphasises how they were 'part of the fabric of industrial relations' and describes anonymous threatening letters, effigy-burning or machine-smashing. He highlights the attack on John Kay's home by workers protesting against his 'flying shuttle' in 1753 and the smashing of **hundreds** of Arkwright's stocking frames in 1779 after failing to secure a minimum wage.

---

[29] Porter, Roy, *"England in the Eighteenth Century"* Penguin, London, (1982)

There is no evidence that any of these incidents resulted in anything but a minor disruption and did nothing to alter or constrain the progress of the industrial revolution.

Origins of the 'Luddites'

From around 1810/1811, groups of men began smashing stocking frames in several parts of the East Midlands, particularly in Nottingham. One version of the myth is that these men were led by Ned Ludd a weaver from Anstey, near Leicester. The story goes that in 1779, either after being whipped for idleness, or after being taunted by local youths, he smashed two knitting frames in what was described as a "fit of passion". Although this story is contentious or a downright lie (and there are several different versions, some said he lived in Robin Hood's old haunt of Sherwood Forest), it is a fact that the gangs setting about frame smashing called themselves 'Luddites' and named their leader as Ned Ludd, General Ludd or Captain Ludd. They even sent threatening letters to frame owners signed by General Ludd. Within the space of three weeks, more than two hundred stocking frames were destroyed.

Some local historians have even suggested that Jeremiah Brandreth, later to lead the Pentrich Rising, was the 'General Ludd' in the Nottingham area.

In March, 1811, several attacks were taking place every night and the Nottingham authorities had to enrol four hundred special constables to protect the factories. At one stage there were 3,000 troops billeted in and around Nottingham and at a time when they could have been needed beyond our shores. To help catch the culprits, the Prince Regent offered £50 to anyone "giving information on any person or persons wickedly breaking the frames". There were reports of frame breaking in Ilkeston and Swanwick in 1810/1811, the latter probably involving and, perhaps, led by Thomas Bacon. Whilst the authorities seemed to be aware of Bacon's involvement he was never arrested.

The Government took the situation seriously to the extent that in February 1812 Spencer Perceval proposed that machine-breaking should become a capital offence. The Government chose to take a repressive posture rather than a sympathetic analysis of the issues involved, probably because there was no machinery or process for consultation and debate. Nevertheless, this enactment was successful in greatly decreasing the destruction of knitting frames and order was restored to such an extent that a second act replacing the death penalty by a maximum sentence of deportation was possible.

Whilst weavers saw the new powered machines as one of the main cause of their unemployment others sought any pretence to demonstrate against what they saw as their deteriorating situation. In actual fact wage reductions, changes in fashion and the collapse of demand played a significant part. The gradual change from wool to cotton over the recent decades also had an impact on their livelihood.

Stocking knitting was predominantly a domestic industry, the stockinger renting his frame from the master and working in his own 'shop' using thread given to him by the master; the finished items were handed back to the master to sell. The frames were therefore scattered round the villages; it was easy for the Luddites to smash a frame and then disappear. Between March 1811 and February 1812 they smashed about a thousand machines at the cost of between £6,000 and £10,000[30].

In June 1812 Lord Sidmouth became Home Secretary, by which time the outbreaks of Luddism had begun to diminish. However in July, parliament set up Secret Committees for the examination of evidence from the 'disturbed areas'. Information had been given to Major Searle, the commander of the South Devon Militia, which was stationed in Sheffield. The informant who was not identified submitted a report part of which said:

"It is the opinion of persons, both in civil and military stations, well acquainted with the state of the country, an opinion grounded upon various

---

[30] See *"The Victorian Web"* http://www.victorianweb.org/history/riots/luddites.html

information from various quarters now before your committee, but which, for obvious reasons, they do not think proper to detail, that the views of some of the persons engaged in these proceedings have extended to revolutionary measures of the most dangerous description.

Their proceedings manifest a degree of caution and organisation which appears to flow from the direction of some persons under whose influence they act . . ."[31]

On the strength of the evidence, the Secret Committees in parliament approved a Bill to preserve the public peace of the 'disturbed districts' and to give additional powers to the magistrates. It passed through parliament and remained in force until 25 March 1813. This was the only way that the government could compensate for the inefficient methods of crime prevention at the time. However, despite the government's fears, there is no conclusive evidence that the activities of the Luddites were politically motivated. This said, it is certainly true that some committed insurrectionists and republicans, such as Bacon and Brandreth, saw the situation as a benefit to their cause.

There was at least some recognition of the pressure on working people when another parliamentary committee heard petitions for relief from the cotton workers and reported to parliament in 1812: however it is clear from this section of the report that the government would do nothing to move from the economic ideas of laissez faire, they reported:

While the Committee fully acknowledge and most deeply lament the great distress of numbers of persons engaged in the cotton manufacture, they are of opinion that no interference of the legislature with the freedom of trade, or with the perfect liberty of every individual to dispose of his time and of his labour in the way and on the terms which he may judge most conducive to his own interest, can take place without violating general principles of the first importance to the prosperity and happiness of the community, without establishing the most pernicious precedent, or without

---

[31] Parliamentary Debates, 1st Series, Vol.23, Col.1036. (1812)

aggravating, after a very short time, the pressure of the general distress, and imposing obstacles against that distress ever being removed[32].

The term '*luddite*' has even found its way into modern English language as 'any opponent of industrial or even artistic change or innovation'.

It is likely that this particular period was when Thomas Bacon made the transition from a local political influence to an activist. He came to the fore as a key figure in machine-breaking in South Wingfield, Pentrich and Swanwick in December 1811 and, particularly, in 1812, 'in the year 1812 he was head of the Luddite Party in Pentrich and Swanwick which did considerable mischief in these places[33]'. It was also believed that he used his experience as a Luddite leader to build up the revolutionary organisation he committed himself to. However, on the other hand, if he had been plotting for 30 years, as he claimed later, perhaps it was the other way round[34]. Despite several references to his involvement, he was never arrested and no official record exists of his activities although it is recorded that Lord Sidmouth knew of his involvement. Doubtless, Bacon's notoriety during this period helped to enhance his reputation as a committed radical and activist.

It would seem that the spell of frame-breaking from late 1811 to 1812/1813 marked the first 'direct action' taken by men from the Pentrich, South Wingfield and Swanwick area. It does not, of course, rule out the possibility that some may have been involved in Luddite activity elsewhere. There were also spates of hay-rick burning from time to time. In fact three locals, George Booth, John Brown and Thomas Jackson were convicted and hanged for burning Colonel William Halton's ricks, the local JP of Alfreton Hall, in August 1817

Conversely, the cause of the Luddite was not always the same as that of the 'radical'. The typical Luddite was a craftsman who believed his likelihood was under threat by labour saving machines and greedy employers. It was

---

[32] Parliamentary Debates, 1st Series, Vol. 20, (1811) Col.609
[33] Treasury Solicitor TS/11/132 quoted in Stevens, Op. Cit.
[34] Stevens, Op. Cit. p. 154

not linked to the wider demands for better representation, reform of parliament or even revolution. However, it did become effective in gathering together large groups of men in the weaving areas of the country. Bacon believed that the success of the Luddites could be extended to the destruction of the government and the constitution.

Whilst frame-breaking was experienced in 1815 and 1816 it was at a reduced level and probably controlled by the fact that it was, for a while, punishable by the death penalty, later reduced to transportation for life.

From a cynical perspective, it has been suggested that the government's knowledge of Bacon's involvement and status in the local radical movement might serve them better by keeping him under observation than by precipitous action. Subsequent facts tend to lend a degree of support to this argument.

One should not under-estimate the effect of the Luddite period as there were several murders, violent beatings, a great deal of damage and a string of hangings. Conversely there is little evidence that the activities resulted in any significant change in the position of the weaver and stockinger.

Local Law Enforcement

During the key periods of our story in central Derbyshire, law enforcement was not as it is to-day, especially at the local level. The key person charged with law enforcement in the county was the **Lord Lieutenant** who was the nominal 'personal representative' of the Monarch and his government in the area and this position came with a great deal of power and influence. He, for we are talking of the seventeenth and eighteenth century, would have an appointed **High Sheriff** as his deputy and maybe a deputy sheriff whose main task would be the hustings and elections for parliament; which were open ballots.

For example, the industrialist Richard Arkwright was knighted and appointed High Sheriff of Derbyshire in 1787. During Thomas Bacon's lifetime the Derbyshire Lord Lieutenants were:

William Cavendish, 4th Duke of Devonshire 21 January 1756 – 1764
John Manners, Marquess of Granby 23 June 1764 – 1766
Lord George Cavendish 17 June 1766 – 1782
William Cavendish, 5th Duke of Devonshire 2 July 1782 – 29 July 1811
William Cavendish, 6th Duke of Devonshire 27 August 1811 – 18 January 1858.

All of these men, who owned substation tracts of the county would have a significant personal interest in maintaining law and order amongst the working class or 'lower orders'.

The Lord Lieutenant would recommend **Justices of the Peace** who would administrator justice at the level below the judge-lead senior courts. JP's could appoint a 'constable' to deal with local issues and the Lord Lieutenant would have a degree of authority over any troops barracked in his area. In addition, the JP's could swear in 'special constables' for specific events or difficult periods. In fact, during the period of the disturbances and Luddite activity many thousands of troops were stationed around England and at a time when they would have been needed elsewhere (refer to the chronology).

The first 'professional' police force was the Bow Street Runners, formed by Henry Fielding in 1742 with the strength of six men at first. The Bow Street Group, the members of which never used the term 'runners', was disbanded in 1839. The Metropolitan Police was formed in 1824 to serve the greater London area. Police forces were established throughput the country in the following decades. It is interesting to note that Derbyshire was one of the last counties to be 'persuaded of the need' to pay for a professional force when it was required to do so in 1857 with 156 warranted officers across the whole county. Most of the senior officers would have been former military officers. Incidentally, it was recommended that junior officers, constables and sergeants, should **not** be recruited from the middle or upper classes, in other words from 'gentlemen'.

Law-breaking was a hazardous occupation during this period; there were hundreds of offences carrying the death penalty. No less than 63 of these were added in the years 1760 – 1810 including petty theft, primitive forms of industrial rebellion such as destroying a silk loom, throwing down fences when commons were enclosed and firing corn ricks[35].

Throughout the period covered by this book, the lack of a trained constabulary and the particular position of the landed gentry in law enforcement required them to acquire their 'information' on law-breaking and 'unacceptable' activities from a variety of sources. It was common to use informants and spies at the local level in addition to the national network operated by government.

The position of the Lord Lieutenant, High Sheriff and JP's in being both the landlord and employer to many of the residents provided them with a particular agenda and the power to extract information readily. For example, informants doubtless watched Thomas Bacon's activities closely and also reported on meeting of secret societies and Hampden Clubs in the area, an explanation of which will be given in the next chapter.

The entire network of radical groups, so-called secret committees and corresponding societies were riddled with spies and, even more insidious, *agents provocateur*, of which there is no more pertinent example than that of the spy William Oliver.

---

[35] Porter (1982), Op. Cit.

8. Radical Societies

Early Societies

According to White (1957)[36], The Derby Society for Political Information held *An Address to the Friends of Free Enquiry and the General Good* in 1792 at The Talbot Inn, Derby. The debate began by quoting Edmund Burke *"We refuse to approach the defects of government with pious awe and trembling solicitude."* One wonders whether Thomas Bacon made the 13 mile walk to attend this meeting. He would be 38 at the time, at the beginning of his radical education and probably discovering Paine's *Rights of Man Pt.2"*. Records of this organisation are held in the National Archives.

The London Corresponding Society

The most famous such organisation was the London Corresponding Society which was formed by Thomas Hardy a shoemaker, John Binns, a plumber, and metropolitan radical, John Frost, an attorney, and a few friends on 25 January 1792 at the Bell Inn, Exeter Street, off the Strand in London. The declared aim of the society was parliamentary reform, especially the expansion of the representation of working class people. In common with many other corresponding societies its membership was predominantly drawn from artisans and working men.

Membership was not limited otherwise than by 'an affirmative reply' to three questions, the most significant being:

"Are you thoroughly persuaded that the welfare of these kingdoms require that every adult person, in possession of his reason, and not incapacitated by crimes, should have a vote for a Member of Parliament?"

---

[36] White, R.J. *"From Waterloo to Peterloo"* Heinemann (1957)

The perceptive reader may notice the use of the words 'every adult person' as opposed to man or male. These words and the implications for female suffrage did not gather any serious consideration for almost a hundred years.

It was widely recognised as the first working-class political organisation. However, Thompson (1963)[37] suggests there were in fact similar groups in Sheffield, Derby, as above, and Manchester before this date.

These societies irritated the establishment with their opposition to the wars with France and were deeply infiltrated by spies. Two LCS representatives were arrested, tried and sentenced to fourteen years transportation. Binns was arrested on several occasions and after his release in 1801, emigrated to America. John Frost received only six months for his sedition. Undaunted, the remaining LCS leaders met with other reformist groups, including the Society for Constitutional Information, in 1794 to discuss a further national convention as well as producing a large number of pamphlets and periodicals.

Another key member was John Thelwell (1764-1834) an apprentice tailor who progressed to being an attorney. After imprisonment for holding seditious meetings, he spent his life touring the country lecturing on Roman history, drawing parallels with contemporary events and offering radical interpretations. He was just the type of speaker who have helped reinforce if not indoctrinate, Bacon's radical views. Finally, in listing these potentially influential speakers we ought to mention Anthony Thistlewood (1774-1820) a revolutionary extremist. He was involved in the Cato Street Conspiracy to destroy the Cabinet. As a direct result he was tried for High Treason, convicted and subsequently hanged and decapitated in 1820.

Not every reformer thought the gentle approach followed by the corresponding societies would succeed. For example, The Rev Christopher Wyvill, regarded as a Yorkshire moderate, in a letter to Major Cartwright dated 16th December 1797 expressed the belief that a reform on the

---

[37] Thompson, E.P. "The making of the English Working Class" Penguin (1963)

principle of universal suffrage *'could not be effected* (sic) *without a Civil War'*.

In May 1794 the government took more action when some of the leaders were arrested and tried for treason in October, but were acquitted by a Grand Jury. The society was not restrained by these efforts and in 1795 there were a number of public meetings, including one near Copenhagen House attended by a few thousand people. Also King George III's carriage was stoned as he went to open a session of parliament. The government responded with the so-called Two Acts - an extension of the treason laws with the Treasonable Practices Act and also the repressive Seditious Meetings Act 1795; detention without trial had already been in force since 1794 when habeas corpus was suspended.

In 1798 the society became increasingly split and in 1799 together with several other radical groups was declared illegal under the Corresponding Societies Act. The LCS effectively ended then, although it maintained a vague, informal existence for a little time after.

Origins of the Hampden Clubs

Major John Cartwright, who's influence on Thomas Bacon is covered in chapter 4, and Thomas Northmore, an English writer, inventor and geologist, who were involved in radical Whig politics, formed The **Hampden Clubs** initially in London in 1812 (they were called 'County Clubs' in some areas). The name came from John Hampden (Cir. 1595 – 1643) an English politician who was one of the leading Parliamentarians involved in challenging the authority of Charles I of England in the run-up to the English Civil War. He stood trial in 1637 for his refusal to be taxed for ship money, and was one of the Five Members whose attempted unconstitutional arrest by King Charles I in the House of Commons of England in 1642 sparked the Civil War.

Major Cartwright, as he liked to be known, certainly dominated the movement from 1813 onwards. A former naval and militia officer with a long record of political activism, he initially toured northwest England to promote the idea of a forum for political debate among 'ordinary people'. In 1813 Cartwright was arrested in Huddersfield while promoting the Clubs. He made a further promotional tour in 1815 encouraging other parliamentary reformers to follow his example. Cartwright's main objective was to unite middle class moderates with radical members of the working class in the cause of parliamentary reform. There had been no similar institutions since the London Corresponding Society was disbanded.

Thompson (1963)[38] has argued: "Major Cartwright defined as early as this the main claims he never swerved. Incapable of compromise, eccentric and courageous, the Major pursued his single-minded course, issuing letters, appeals, and pamphlets, from his seat in Boston, Lincolnshire, surviving trials, tumults, dissension and repression.... before the Napoleonic Wars had ended, he found the first reform societies of a new ear, the Hampton Clubs, in those northern industrial regions where his clerical brother had accelerated other processes of change with his invention of the power-loom."

The first Hampden Club outside of London was formed in 1816 by William Fitton at Royden. Soon afterwards, Samuel Bamford formed one at Middleton and Joseph Healey did the same in Oldham. Later that year John Knight and Joseph Johnson started the Manchester Hampden Club. Other clubs supporting the ideas of Major John Cartwright were also formed in Rochdale, Ashton-under-Lyne and Stockport. Meetings took place once a week and as well as having debates on various political issues; radical newspapers such as the *Manchester Observer*, *Cobbett's Political Register*, the *Black Dwarf* and *Sherwin's Political Register* were read to the members.

---

[38] Thompson, Op. Cit.

'Second Generation' Hampden Clubs

These 'Hampden clubs' were replicated in less prestigious locations and appeared throughout the country, including Pentrich, Alfreton, Ripley amongst other towns and villages in Derbyshire. In the years prior to 1817, many were concentrated in the midlands and the northern counties and were closely associated with the popular movements for social and political reform that arose in the years following the end of the Napoleonic wars.

Thomas Bacon was a leading organiser of the Pentrich Hampden Club, meeting at the White Horse, and was known to visit and speak at many other similar organisations. He also regularly attended the club held at the Cock Inn, Ripley.

Another club visited by Bacon was the Heanor Hampden Club, the Chairman and leading man being Thomas Allens at The Nags Head. It was later to meet in a large room which used to be a Methodist meeting house, belonging to Samuel Weston of Tag Hill near Heanor.

The clubs were forced underground and eventually disbanded in the face of legislation and pressure from the authorities. There were Hampden Clubs in many local villages which continued meeting; several of the key personalities in the Pentrich Rising were members and were believed to have taken oaths of secrecy. The point at which these talking clubs turned to planning the overthrow of the Government is debateable. However, it is certain that they did give a degree of credibility to local radicals and the feeling that they were not alone in their radical views. The Hampden Clubs did provide a point of access at which anyone seeking to influence radical activity could apply pressure. Unfortunately, they also provided a convenient point of access for spies seeking information about active radicals and their plans.

In many areas they provided a stock of relevant literature for the aspiring reformer and some even had reading rooms.

It is a fact that there were a growing number of radical thinkers inspired by events in America, France and, to a lesser extent, England[39]. Many of whom would be classed as members of the aristocracy although perhaps not of the 'top drawer'.

A report of the House of Commons referred particularly to the Hampden clubs as being:

" . . . avowed machines of revolution, and also spoke with mixed feelings of suspicion and alarm concerning the activity of the leaders; of the great numbers of people they were inducing to take the oaths which bound them to the cause they were championing; and the means that had been afforded to attain the objects they had in view, which were declared to be the overthrow of all rights of property and all the National institutions, to introduce a system of Government that would bring about a state of insecurity, anarchy and plunder".

Cartwright's vision of The Hampden club was originally for the purpose of introducing Parliamentary reform and amongst some of the leading men were to be found Lord Cochrane, Sir Francis Burdett, Major Cartwright, Cobbett, and others. As these gentlemen were the owners of large properties, and that by encouraging and sanctioning such a policy they would be sacrificing a great portion of their possessions, it is only fair to them to say that the policy resorted to by some persons who were probably connected with these clubs was not countenanced by those gentlemen and many advised the people of the country to refrain from violence of any kind.

It seems clear that the locally formed Hampden Clubs were not strictly formed on Cartwright's original format and many used these organisations to further their radical aspirations. This was certainly the case in Pentrich and the surrounding area.

---

[39] Cobbett, Hunt and the Frenchman Rousseau amongst others already mentioned

In actual fact, in some of the rather obscure parts of the country there had been clubs formed which contemplated the ridiculous idea of taking possession of local properties, but these did not emanate from the original Hampden Clubs. It was thought that committees of both Houses of Parliament had been misled with regard to this matter probably by their spies seeking to profit on their 'payment by results' employment.

Secret Committees

There were many so-called 'secret committees' formed on both sides of the political divide. Acutely aware of the sensitivities of their activities many gathered together in these Secret Committees. In parliament there were secret committees of each house who reported to the Home Secretary and Prime Minister for the examination of evidence from the 'disturbed areas' around the country; but not to their full representative houses. Many members would be unaware of their work!

On 22nd May 1814 the Town Clerk of Nottingham informed the Home Office of a secret committee to combat the activities of the stockingers Union, presumably frame-breaking. The Town Clerk wrote to the Home Office in a letter containing the following paragraph:

I am sure you are aware how essential Secrecy is to the Success of our measures & how imperious a Duty it is upon me as the Secretary of this Committee. I have however the greatest pleasure of stating to you that the Members of this Committee are Gentlemen of the greatest respectability & upon whom collectively & individually Government may [repose] the most unlimited Confidence. I write to you my Dear Sir entirely from myself with a view to your Information & [certainly] for the Information thro' your medium of Lord Sidmouth and Invite on your part any confidential communication of the wishes of Government in relation to this Committee—I have reason to think that you will before this have reason to know that this Committee has not been idle since its appointm' I can assure you it has occupied a great deal of my time.—I am sure you will perceive that it is essential to my Situation you should have the Goodness to withhold from every Person whatever connected with the corresponding Committee in London any letter of a confidential nature from me which may have relation to the secret Committee here or the communications made by them to the London Committee.

Using the same title, perhaps to confuse, local radical groups formed secret committees. For example, the Nottingham Secret Committee, chaired by the needlemaker William Stevens, was active during this period. Thomas Bacon was a regular visitor as were some of his Pentrich / South Wingfield colleagues such as Ludlam, Turner and the Weightmans. This committee served to co-ordinate insurrectionary activity in the town of Nottingham and its surrounding area. It is known William Oliver visited from time to time. It may be a fair assumption to make that, if Bacon was seeking an alternative leader for the Pentrich Rising, a suitable candidate would be found here, see chapter fifteen. It is still unclear whether Brandreth ever met Oliver. Nevertheless logic suggests, in view of Oliver's involvement, if Jeremiah Brandreth did meet William Oliver, which some have denied, it would have been at the Nottingham Secret Committee.

Meetings of the Nottingham Secret Committee were being held during this period at the 'Three Salmons Inn', Nottingham. These were attended by Jeremiah Brandreth and George Crabtree, a Nottingham printer. In fact, Crabtree regularly visited Pentrich and had met Oliver, whilst he was posing as the 'London Delegate'.

9. Growing Discontent

The entire period of Thomas Bacon's adult life had its problems with riots and disturbances, after gathering all available and relevant statistics, Gault (2009)[40] produced a schedule that suggested that from 1790 to 1815 there were between 20 and 30 significant riots each year. However, there were notable years, in 1800 there were 85 riots, 1801-55 and 1810-40. The highest number recorded during this period was in 1790, at a time when the French Revolution was at its height, with around 130 riots were recorded in England. These facts should have served to focus the government's attention on efforts to address at least some of the issues of the lower orders. They seemed to have done little more than enhance the case for harsher legislation whilst continuing with their *'laissez-faire'* philosophy.

The years of 1815 and 1816 served to deepen the levels of discontent and, in every likelihood, combined to move some from minor disturbances, local frame-breaking and rick-burning, to discussing plans for a full-blown insurrection.

The Prince Regent had been installed on a permanent basis since 1812 and his profligate life-style based in London and the ornate Brighton Pavilion was being to become common knowledge. One of his closest acolytes was the reprobate George 'Beau' Brummell; that is until they quarrelled over gambling debts in 1818. Some of the politically motivated newspapers carried cartoons of the obese Prince Regent amongst his hedonistic friends.

Many were beginning to think that there might just be a better way. The more perceptive had seen how America and France had taken a route away from rule by and for the benefit of the monarch, the upper classes and the landed gentry. Maybe a republic was the answer? Did it seem that the 'so-called' democracy of the present was not serving the working class? Furthermore, writing critical papers, presenting petitions, delivering inspirational speeches had never been the favourite way of the lower orders and, by any realistic measure, it did not appear to be effective.

---

[40] Gaunt, op. cit. (p.99)

Thomas Bacon and a few close friends, like Ludlam and Turner, began to persuade others that they could and should aspire to a better world. That their life should not be as miserable and unfortunate as it appeared to be. Furthermore, similar feelings were coming to the fore around the country although perhaps not as many as the Pentrich group were led to believe.

A Dangerous Mix

According to Halevy (1924)[41] in the period 1811 to 1814 Luddite Associations were spreading disorder throughout Yorkshire, Lancashire, Derbyshire, Nottingham and Cheshire. They were predominantly loose unions of workman more than political associations. They had no political creed or programme although many broke the law by taking oaths of allegiance and secrecy. Their aim, certainly the aim of the vast majority, was the destruction of machinery and factories and not a political revolution. Whereas Cartwright's associations (and those of others) were peaceable and, generally speaking harmless; they were seeking parliamentary reform particularly universal male suffrage. However, the fear was that should the day arrive when the two would unite creating a situation far more dangerous than 1795 when riots and disturbances were at their highest. Of course, the French Revolution and 'Madame Guillotine' were still in the minds of the ruling class.

It was well established that the White Horse Pentrich, where the landlady was Tommy Bacon's sister Nancy Weightman, had a wide reputation as a meeting point for radical sympathisers in the surrounding area. Other public houses in the north and midlands gained a similar notoriety.

Many genuinely thought that the time had come to take direct action and, furthermore, that it was the right thing to do. As far as the reports of meeting in and around Pentrich and South Wingfield go, there was no-one promoting an alternative course of action. Even the curate of Pentrich Church, Rev Hugh Wolstenholme, contrary to most of his contemporaries,

---

[41] Halevy, Elie *"A History of the English People in the 19th Century"* vol. 1 England in 1815, Ernest Benn Ltd, (1924)

was a supporter of the radical course having been brought up in a well-known radical family in Yorkshire. In addition, a more sympathetic approach may have been taken by the growing number of Methodists Chapels.

A Developing Situation

There had been poor harvests before, 1794-95 and 1799-1800 for example, but the years of 1815–1816 were as bad as any and added to the usual pressures on the working class. There was even snow in Derbyshire on 7th June 1816. Subsequent findings have added credence to the theory that the poor weather might have been caused by the massive eruption on Mount Tambora in Indonesia and the immense dust cloud encircling the globe.

Thousands of soldiers were returning from the Napoleonic War and after the successes at Waterloo, many were looking for their old jobs back or seeking work in the new factories. Those who could not find work or those too disabled to work became a financial burden on their parish. In addition, there were many families in poverty because their bread winner did not return for the War. There over 300,000 British troops killed or missing in the 1803-1815 conflict. The national economy suffered badly from the expense of the war and the country's debt was high.

Income tax had been imposed to finance the war and following on Pitt's promise to remove it as soon as possible changes were made. The burden fell on indirect taxes and on the domestic economies of the lower orders. Although not reported on a formal basis, it has been suggested that crime, particularly theft, increased.

Lord Liverpool, who succeeded Perceval as Prime Minister in 1812 after his assassination by a disgruntled London merchant, faced considerable problems – post-war debt, parliamentary reform and Catholic emancipation amongst others. He also had to deal with the health of George III and the unfortunate reputation and dubious leadership skills of the Prince Regent.

The Spa Fields Riots, 2 December 1816

After the end of the French Wars, it became increasingly clear that England was suffering from great social, economic and political upheavals. Many of these problems would have occurred eventually but had been speeded up by the effects of the French Wars on the industrial economy and the countryside. For example and at a local level, Butterley Company suffered loss of orders for cannon, ammunition, etc. Other changes came from natural growth and pressure on burgeoning towns. The distress and discontent caused by these enormous changes were manifested in a series of events in the period 1811-19. One of these was the Spa Fields riots at Islington, London. Another, of course, would be the Pentrich Rising.

The first Spa Fields meeting, on 15 November 1816, attracted about 10,000 people and passed off peacefully in the main. Its official object was to seek popular support for the delivery of a petition to the Prince Regent, requesting electoral reform and relief from hardship and distress. Henry 'Orator' Hunt accepted the invitation and then visited his friend William Cobbett who warned Hunt that the meeting could be dangerous. Cobbett omitted to tell Hunt that he, too, had been invited but had declined. Henry Hunt addressed the meeting and was elected to deliver the petition, along with Sir Francis Burdett.

Hunt spoke from the window of a public house; he wore his white top hat, a symbol of radicalism and the 'purity of his cause'. Behind him flew a tricolour flag and a Cap of Liberty. Hunt waxed lyrical about the evils of high prices and over-taxation, the greed of the borough-mongers and sinecurists and the necessity for parliamentary reform. The meeting was peaceful; Hunt made no appeal to force but he did advise his audience to sign a petition 'before physical force was applied'. The petition embodied the full radical programme of the day:

- Universal (male) suffrage
- Annual general elections
- Secret ballots

In his speech, Hunt said that he knew the superiority of mental over physical force; nor would he counsel any resort to the latter till the former had been found ineffectual. Before physical force was applied to, it was their duty to petition, to remonstrate, to call aloud for timely reformation. Those who resisted the just demands of the people were the real friends of confusion and bloodshed . . . but if the fatal day should be destined to arrive, he assured them that if he knew anything of himself; he would not be found concealed behind a counter, or sheltering himself in the rear[42].

Hunt and Burdett were elected to take the petition to the Prince Regent. Burdett declined the honour; he and Hunt fell out over the former's refusal to present the petition. Hunt accused Burdett of running away and said that he abandoned any idea that Burdett would ever do *'anything effectually to relieve the people'*. Hunt then made two futile attempts to present the petition to Prince George and twice was refused admission to the Regent's presence. The petition was eventually presented by Lord Cochrane but received little support in parliament.

The organisers did not know that a small group, led by Thomas Spence who opposed the British government, had planned to encourage rioting and then seize control of the government by taking the Tower of London and the Bank of England.

On 2 December another meeting was held at Spa Fields to protest at the treatment that Hunt had received. This meeting, attracting around 20,000 people, degenerated into the Spa Fields riot. Hunt was late for the meeting and was driving down Cheapside when he was met by a man called Castle who told Hunt that he was too late, that 'the people' had taken the Tower of London. When Hunt arrived at Spa Fields, he saw a waggon in the middle of the crowd that was decorated with banners, one of which said 'the brave soldiers are our friends'. In the waggon stood Dr James Watson and his son, also James, Arthur Thistlewood and other men who met at the Cock and Mulberry Tree public houses where the Spenceans gathered. The younger

---

[42] taken from E.P. Thompson, The Making of the English Working Class (Penguin Books, 1968), p.685

James Watson jnr was pontificating from Camille Desmoulin's cafe-table exhortation to the patriots of Paris before the storming of the Bastille:

If they will not give us what we want, shall we not take it? Are you willing to take it? Will you go and take it? If I jump down amongst you, will you come and take it?

Watson then jumped down, picked up a tricolour and set off for the Tower of London. Some sailors supplied the muscle and a gunsmith's shop on Snow Hill was robbed to provide weapons. One of the sailors subsequently was executed for his part in the riot although he was probably the scapegoat rather than a dangerous radical; he had just arrived in London having been demobilised after spending years fighting in the French Wars. A pedestrian was killed by the mob which then made for the Royal Exchange where they were confronted by Alderman Shaw and seven constables. Shaw did not see any weapons and arrested three of the leaders of the mob. By nightfall, order had been restored in the city. The incident has been described as "*five fanatics hounded on by a spy*": the government had the leaders charged with High Treason. They were acquitted when Castle, the informer, presented his evidence.

The role of the spy Castle was exposed by Wetherell, a High Tory:

"If you bear in mind who is the principal (I should say the only) witness in this case - a man of the name of Castle; if you bear in mind what he has proved to have done in the course of these transactions; if you bear in mind for whom he is a witness, from what place he comes, what he has been, and what he now is ... you will hereafter consider whether Mr. Castle is not the man who has made these persons his dupes; whether he has not alone invented, organised and framed the whole of the projects which he represents were moulded into a system of conspiracy; whether, according to every fair and rational presumption, he is not the author and parent of all these transactions, forming an ideal conspiracy for purposes of his own."[43]

---

[43] State Trials, Vol. 32, pp.421-422

However, the incident completed the alienation of Burdett from the Hunt/Cobbett/Cartwright leadership and convinced Lord Sidmouth that there was a revolution in the making in the provinces of England. This is made clear in the Report of the Secret Committee into the Disturbed State of the Country, February 1817[44].

Attempts have been made, in various parts of the country, as well as in the metropolis, to take advantage of the distress in which the labouring and manufacturing classes of the community are at present involved, to induce them to look for immediate relief, not only in a reform of Parliament on the plan of universal suffrage and annual election, but in a total overthrow of all existing establishments, and in a division of the landed, and extinction of the funded property of the country.

In reaction to these events, the government passed the so called "Gagging Acts" in February and March 1817, see chapter 12.

The series of events, probably emanating from the impact of the French Revolution in 1789, resulted in suspicion and mistrust. Many thought that talk and the submission of petitions to parliament would be pointless.

---

[44] Parliamentary Debates, 1st Series, vol. 35, (1817) col.438

10. The Crown and Anchor, London

Proof, if proof were needed, that Thomas Bacon was a significant figure in the national radical movement is provided by his attendance at the delegates meeting held at the Crown and Anchor Tavern, Arundel Street, London on 22nd January 1817. A meeting which some termed the 'delegates' convention' was chaired by Major Cartwright and was ostensibly to discuss the presentation of a petition; many of the delegates would be harbouring more severe agendas. It was probably one of the first occasions when the likes of Cartwright, Burdett and others came face to face with some of the regional delegates.

The Crown and Anchor tavern was located in London's bustling central business area of the Strand, opposite Christopher Wren's seventeenth-century church of St Clement Danes and only a short distance from London's focus of power in Westminster. From the perspective of the White Horse public house in Pentrich or the Cock Inn at Ripley, the Crown and Anchor was a very different place. This meeting probably marked the beginning of the endgame that was to terminate in the Pentrich Rising and the realisation, or perhaps the demolition, of Thomas Bacon's dreams.

It may be worthwhile pausing a while to consider the Crown and Anchor itself. Entering the building from Arundel Street, visitors were greeted by an elegant foyer, paved with stone and dominated by four large Doric columns, which supported a gallery above. The entry was light and spacious, produced by a large lantern that hung overhead. The tavern's considerable kitchen facilities were located on the ground floor, providing convenient access to the aptly named Large Dining Room, which could seat upwards of 500 guests. The room was simply but elegantly appointed. Enriched carved cornices circled the ceiling, which featured two large moulded centrepieces of carved flowers supporting the room's chandeliers. Two substantial fireplaces framed with marble and wood dressings provided winter warmth. Festoons (carved chains of flowers, leaves or ribbons hung in curves) cascaded from the walls of an arched recess at the western end of the room, with the walls adorned with a frieze of eight panels.

A prodigious staircase constructed of stone, framed by continuous ornamental iron rails and topped with mahogany handrails, led to the upper floors. Ascending the staircase to the second floor, visitors to the tavern could momentarily catch their breath in the small second-floor lobby—described as a 'large well hole', lit both by natural light drawn into the space by two conical skylights and, in the evenings, by a huge lantern raised six feet, six inches (1.98 m) high. The lobby provided an area for guests to assemble before making their entrance into the Crown and Anchor's premium asset: the 'Great Assembly Room'. The room was one of the largest available in the metropolis, measuring an immense 2969 sq ft (276 sq m) and was reportedly capable of hosting concerts, balls and banquets for at least 2000 people. The room was elegantly appointed with chandeliers, marble fireplaces and intricately carved architraves and cornices, and the centre of the immense ceiling was garnished with an ornate domical centrepiece of formidable proportions which grasped an enormous chandelier. Like the Large Dining Room, here an enriched moulded frieze and cornice encircled the entire room with 'ornamental panels, medallions and festoons' featured on four walls. These were further detailed with Doric pilasters mirroring the facade of the building. A raised music gallery for orchestras was situated at the western end of the room, surrounded by iron railings and supported by three fluted Doric columns. Three substantial arched windows at the eastern end of the room allowed for illumination by daylight.[45]

Very few of the working class revolutionaries, if any, would have seen such a sight! It must have been an awe-inspiring vision for Thomas Bacon of Pentrich. It would be interesting to take the position of a fly on the wall as Bacon and the delegates from the midlands and north entered this building. Of course there were working class people in London but *they* would not be entering this building by the front door!

The status of the tavern as an analogue to Parliament is particularly evident in the choice of the Crown and Anchor for meetings of national assemblies of plebeian reformers. In January 1817, several newspapers reported on the

---

[45] Pavolin, Christina *"Radical Spaces; Venues of Popular Politics in London 1790-1845"* Australian National University, Canberra (2010)

meeting of 'delegates from various Petitioning Bodies in Great Britain, for Reform in Parliament'. Delegates travelled from small and large towns across England, including Bristol, Norwich, Middleton, Lynn, Manchester, Lancashire and Liverpool. Radical luminary Major Cartwright stood in as the delegate for Glasgow, Scotland's radical stronghold. Before starting the meeting, the delegates from Westminster—Hunt, William Cobbett and Mr Brooks—ceremoniously received 'vouchers' from each of the country delegates entitling them to represent the reformers of their towns. The representatives of the regional areas had assembled at the request of Major Cartwright and Jones Burdett (brother of Sir Francis) as representatives of the Hampden Club, a network of reform groups initiated by Cartwright to advance the cause of parliamentary reform. Cartwright and Sir Francis Burdett had been deputed by the Hampden Club to:

'lay before the assembled delegates of the petitioning bodies of the country in favour of reform, the heads of a bill for that measure, which it was intended in March next to lay before the whole body of that society, previous to its being submitted to Parliament'.

The petition subsequently submitted by Lord Cochrane had thousands of signatures but was defeated in the Commons by 265 votes to 77.

The Hampden Club members were generally regarded as moderate middle-class reformers and the bill reflected their temperate approach to parliamentary reform. The bill declared that members of the House of Commons should be elected by householders; that the counties and cities be divided into electoral districts, with each district returning one member; and that elections should be conducted annually.

The Crown and Anchor meeting debated and discussed the three tenets of the resolution for hours. Finally, they rejected the notion of limiting suffrage to householders (owners of property), voting by a majority to instead support Hunt's resolution for universal male suffrage. Buoyed by his success, Hunt pressed further. Despite vocal opposition from Cobbett, he convinced the meeting to support vote by ballot, which was also carried. With two blows against moderate reform measures, the more radical members of the meeting pushed on. The delegate from Manchester (or Leeds), Joseph Mitchell, launched the third strike when his proposal that 'property ought form no part of a Member of Parliament's qualifications' as 'virtue and talents were sufficient' was carried by a 'considerable majority'. The democratic processes in the Crown and Anchor altered the original proposal to such a degree that the meeting agreed to omit any reference whatsoever to the Hampden Club in the bill.

Whether Cartwright or James Burdett anticipated the strength of the venue's radical temper is unclear, as is their reaction to the viperous attack on the club launched by Cobbett. Though he held the individual members of the club such as Cartwright and the Burdetts in the 'highest regard', Cobbett nevertheless insisted that 'there was not, if it were possible to describe them, a body of the dirtiest scavengers in England that he could more sincerely despise than that very society in its collective capacity'.

Despite these obvious hostilities (which others at the meeting shared with Cobbett), the key point in this episode is that the Hampden Club sought approval for its reform bill first within the Crown and Anchor meeting. The Hampden Club clearly considered that the sanction of those gathered at the tavern was crucial to the endorsement of the club as a leading exponent of reform in the country and a way of legitimising the submission of the Bill to Parliament. The people's parliament, however, would have none of it unless the moderates in the Hampden Club embraced more sweeping and much deeper political change.[46]

The meeting produced a swift reaction from The Times. *'Ill friends are they to parliamentary reform'*, they chastised, *'who adopt such a course as this'*. The newspaper was most concerned that it was 'not aware till after the event had taken place' that the group had assembled. Taking issue with the 'secrecy' of the event, they questioned the representative nature of a group who met in that same 'dark, suspicious, and irresponsible manner' by which they had proposed parliamentary members be chosen—'that is, by ballot'. Significantly, then, even *The Times* now expected the Crown and

---

[46] Pavolin (2010) Op. Cit.

Anchor to operate as an open and accessible part of the public sphere. They viewed amended resolutions as too extreme for the good of the country, charging the group with 'endeavouring, so far as in them lies, not only to overthrow the constitution directly and openly, but to subvert the very nature and habits of Englishmen'.

The Crown and Anchor could boast of a conspicuous history with regard to radicalism over many years.

It should be noted that the 'Mr Mitchell' (Joseph Mitchell) referred to in the debates was the same man who accompanied Bacon in some of the later meetings in spring 1817.

One can only imagine what Thomas Bacon made of this experience and how he relayed the proceedings to the men at Pentrich and South Wingfield on his return. Did he add a personal 'twist' to the content of the debate or did he faithfully pass on all he could remember. It would certainly give a degree of kudos to his standing in the community.

11. International Distractions

Throughout the entire period of Thomas Bacon's life the British government was pre-occupied with a series of international events, wars and catastrophes many running concurrently and all expensive. To look back to the mid and late eighteenth century is to see a very different governmental structure to what we see to-day. The Monarch was much more involved in policy making and decision taking than in modern times and was even able to appoint senior ministers and key post-holders to follow his particular philosophy. Throughout this entire period all senior politicians were male and all were from the upper or middle classes until the twentieth century; in fact the first female back-bench MP, Nancy Astor did not enter parliament until 1919 (there was a female Sinn Fein in 1918 but she did not take her seat).

For the entirety of Bacon's life the country was controlled by the upper classes, the so-called 'landed gentry'. It is true to say the industrial revolution did provide opportunities for merchant princes and other entrepreneurs to amass large fortunes and many found their way into parliament. However, it was after Bacon's transportation that any significant changes began to be seen in the real and practical influence of working people in Britain.

American War of Independence

When Thomas Bacon was born in 1754, George II reigned and was succeeded by his grandson George III in October 1760. Britain was in the middle of the Seven Years War with France which, by way of a change, was fought in and around North America and not Europe. It is recognised that George III had a less militaristic nature than his grandfather. However, all this would doubtless have passed Thomas Bacon by, he was enjoying his short childhood in Derbyshire. This war was settled in Britain's favour in 1763 but with the burden of a greatly increased national debt.

Britain's First Empire, the thirteen colonies of North America, was then established but destined not to last. The reasons are complex and there are different versions, of course; rule at a distance, openly favouring a private company (The East India Company) and a taxation system against which many of the new Americans objected to, often couched in the 'catchphrase' **no taxation without representation.** This was only one of a series of factors resulting in the War of Independence from 1775. Space precludes an analysis of the war but supporting a war across an ocean, interference from disgruntled settlers, frustrated Native Americans and the actions of France and Spain, proved to be quite a burden both in men and finance.

Back home many sympathised with the American rebels. British confidence had been dented and added momentum to those seeking reform of the parliamentary system. Although Britain suffered financially as well as politically, France was in a worse state – a state that added to the demand for change cross the Channel.

The Irish Problem

Throughout this period, England was struggling with the Irish who were inspired by the American example in their demands for self-determination. One can only imagine the extent to which Bacon took an interest in these affairs. He was approaching his thirties, he could read and, undoubtedly, some newspapers and pamphlets were being circuiting. Even the lower orders were known to pontificate about Pitt becoming Prime Minister, the national debt and the developing madness of George III. In actual fact, medical research discovered that the illness of George III was not merely madness but most probably porphyria, brought on by a kidney disorder. Modern medicine could have controlled this disease. As an aside, it would be an interested but purely academic discussion to conceive how control of the symptoms of his illness might have changed history!

French Revolution

The French Revolution (1789-1799) developed into a process to reform and to restructure the manner in which France was governed. Probably even more so than in Britain, France was organised for the benefit of the wealthy, a series of three 'estates' set the class structure into a rigid format with the King at the top and all-powerful whilst the taxes were levied on the 'third estate' – those at the bottom! The Revolution was centred on Paris, with support from provisional cities, and resulted in a great many men and women being dragged to the guillotine. The mob attacked the Bastille, which was a royal prison similar to the Tower of London, with great celebration. However, they found only seven prisoners inside the prison. In 1793 Louis XVI and his Queen were sent to the guillotine. One can imagine the ice cold blasts of insurrection circulating around the Royal Palaces and corridors of power in London! France did find itself with a more stable government in 1795, the Directory, and eventually the rise to prominence of a diminutive young Corsican soldier, Napoleon Bonaparte.

The French Revolution destabilised much of Europe and resulted in the Revolutionary Wars which lasted until 1802. Thereafter, with a short break for breath, the Napoleonic Wars continued until 1815.

The situation across the channel was closely observed by British reformers. Charles James Fox, the prominent Whig opponent of George III and Pitt, speaking of the French Revolution, said, "How much the greatest event it is that ever happened in the world and how much the best." However, Fox's friend Edmund Burke said, in his *"Reflections on the Revolution in France"*, warned that the revolution was a violent rebellion against tradition and proper authority, motivated by utopian, abstract ideas disconnected from reality, which would lead to anarchy and eventual dictatorship.

Thomas Paine, one of Bacon's inspirations, had found his way from America to France and published his *"The Rights of Man"* in response to Burke, asserting the maxim that people alone were entitled to judge who should rule over them.

The 'activities' in France established or revived the societies seeking reform in Britain. Charles Grey, a follower of Charles Fox, founded the 'Friends of the People'. As mentioned previously, Thomas Hardy created the 'London Corresponding Society'.

The situation in France and the developing feelings for reform would not have gone unnoticed even in the backwoods of central Derbyshire. It is suggested that around this time, when Bacon was in his thirties and forties, he developed or certainly refined, his radical feelings and, possibly, a desire for revolution.

Whilst I have not included all the international activities, this brief overview provides some indication of the state of affairs at a time when Prince Regent was taking the reins from his father, George III, during his illness. Early outbreaks of Luddism occurred during the French Wars and were seen by the government as clear evidence of disaffection amongst the lower orders. Furthermore, in 1809 the war with Spain was not going well.

In 1812 the government probably had even more reasons to be fearful:

- a large part of the army was overseas, mainly in the Peninsular with Wellington;
- the country was fighting not only the French but also the Americans
- England was experiencing the worst trade depression since the 1760s and
- people were suffering great hardship, as evidenced by Luddite actions, the Sheffield riots of 1812 and elsewhere.

Whilst not making any judgement on the government's domestic actions during the period 1800-1817, it must have been extremely difficult to maintain good order throughout the country without the use of repressive legislation, troops that could have been better used elsewhere and, of course, a small army of spies.

12. Legislation

Throughout our general period of interest, the lifetime and radicalisation of Thomas Bacon, there were numerous key pieces of primary legislation impacting on the industrial context and associated events. Some of the more significant acts are listed below.

In addition, government regularly used a form of secondary, delegated legislation or 'Orders in council' to implement decisions made by the King (or Prince Regent) with his senior ministers, in theory during a formally constituted Privy Council meeting, or a secret committee.

A key point on the use of 'Orders in Council' is that they were made relatively quickly and without the full parliamentary discussion and approval. They should, of course, only be used to exercise powers given to them under primary legislation i.e. an Act of Parliament.

Protection of Stocking Frames, etc. Act 1788

This Act was passed in 1788 and aimed at increasing the penalties for the deliberate disruption of the activity of mechanical looms (stocking frames). Section one made failure to return frames that had been hired from their owner punishable with a fine, whilst section two made unlawfully disposing of hired frames punishable with imprisonment, and section three made the purchaser equally culpable if he or she knew the frames were not the property of the seller. The final and most strongly worded section of the Act, section four, made the outright destruction of the frames a felony punishable by 7 to 14 years transportation. The Act also included the same penalty for entering by force with the intent to destroy frames or their associated paraphernalia. It was established in later case law that theft of items integral to the correct functioning of the machines (even if they were not damaged) was sufficient to meet the threshold for the Act.

One can see that the tactic of frame-breaking and other disruptive behaviour was established long before Thomas Bacon and his friends were involved. But, as discussed elsewhere, the reasons were localised and related to employment rather than higher 'political motives'.

The Act described itself as a response to the malicious theft of frames, and the propensity for "discontents ... and other disorderly persons [to] have assembled in a riotous and tumultuous manner and have destroyed or materially damaged great numbers of stocking frames". Daniel Coke, Member of Parliament for Nottingham, spoke on behalf of the bill in the Commons, citing disturbances in the town and pointing to previous legislation aimed at similar disruption in the wool trade. Coke originally proposed that machine-breaking carry the death penalty, but was later forced to abandon this, seeing the request "overwhelmingly rejected" by Parliament. The Act was eventually passed and received royal assent on 25 June 1788.

The Treason Act 1790

Whilst not really within our area of interest, this Act, which abolished burning at the stake as the penalty for women convicted of high treason, petty treason and abetting, procuring or counselling petty treason, and replaced it with hanging and drawing, does give a feel for the context in which people lived.

Habeas Corpus

A writ of habeas corpus is a summons with the force of a court order; it is addressed to the custodian (a prison official for example) and demands that a prisoner be taken before the court, and that the custodian present proof of authority, allowing the court to determine whether the custodian has lawful authority to detain the prisoner. If the custodian is acting beyond his or her authority, then the prisoner must be released. Any prisoner, or another person acting on his or her behalf, may petition the court, or a judge, for a writ of habeas corpus. It is used to challenge the official powers when they detain a person without trial. It has always been a key safe-guard in any 'free' society and can be traced back to the Magna Carta.

However, the right to claim Habeas Corpus was suspended on many occasions during this period in times of 'tension or disturbances' only to be reinstated shortly afterwards and then, of course, suspended yet again when the government thought it wise or convenient to do so.

The Seditious Meetings Act 1795

Approved in November 1795, was the second of the well-known "Two Acts" (also known as the "Gagging Acts" or the "Grenville and Pitt Bills"), the other being the Treason Act 1795. Its purpose was to restrict the size of public meetings to fifty persons. It also required a magistrate's license for lecturing and debating halls where admission was charged and politics discussed.

This legislation was reasonably effective. However, provided that Jacobin alehouse clubs were restricted to fifty persons at any one time and avoided corresponding, they were able to dodge the Seditious Meetings Act. Also, action against individuals for seditious, treasonous or blasphemous words was hindered as spies and shorthand writers could not easily transcribe undiscovered in such an environment. Alehouse debaters could convey anti-establishment sentiments in oblique ways that were difficult to prosecute in a court of law.

In a period of revolution in Europe, the British Parliament attempted to avoid any seditious movement in the kingdoms. The period from 1790-1800 was one of intense lectures and public speeches in defence of political reformation, which, for the similarities with the French Revolution principles, were usually named "Jacobinic meetings". One of the most famous preachers in the period was John Thelwall, who interpreted the "Two Acts" as a 'violence' against him and his teachings. His meetings used to reach a large number of people and, after the approval of the acts, were disturbed by many legalists who wished to see the law being respected. The "Seditious Meetings Act" stated that any place, like a room or building, where political meetings took place, with the purpose of discussing the injustice of any law, constitution, government and policy of the kingdoms, must be declared a house of disorder and punished.

The Treason Act 1795

Sometimes referred to as the Treasonable and Seditious Practices Act, this was one of the Two Acts introduced by the British government in the wake of the stoning of King George III on his way to open Parliament in 1795, the other being the Seditious Meetings Act 1795, see above. The Act made it high treason to "within the realm or without compass, imagine, invent, devise or intend death or destruction, or any bodily harm tending to death or destruction, maim or wounding, imprisonment or restraint, of the person of ... the King." This was derived from the Sedition Act 1661, which had expired. The 1795 Act was originally a temporary Act which was to expire when George III died, but it was made permanent by the Treason Act 1817.

Unlawful Oaths Act 1797

The Act was passed in the aftermath of the Spithead and Nore naval mutinies of that year and aimed at clandestine political associations and 'ad hoc' agreements such as those which had bound several of the mutineers. It was, incidentally, also used against the Tolpuddle Martyrs in 1830's.

Unlawful Societies Act 1799

It was this Act that saw the first statute "for the more effectual suppression of societies established for seditious and treasonable purposes"; once enacted it affected all societies whose members were required to take an oath not authorised by law, shall be deemed "unlawful combinations." It encompassed workers combinations and also created issues for Freemasons.

Combination Act 1799

This first Act, also known as the Unlawful Combination of Workmen Act, prompted by a 'wildcat' strike of millwrights, prohibited trade unions and included a general ban on collective bargaining by British workers. Many saw it has an immediate and 'knee-jerk' reaction to the French Revolution.

Combination Act 1800

The second Act was somewhat of a 'tidying-up' of the previous one. Offences included entering into contracts for the purpose of improving conditions of employment or calling, or attending a meeting for such a purpose and of attempting to persuade another person not to work or to effuse to work with another worker.

The jurisdiction was given to local JP's who could order up to 3 months imprisonment. A similar prohibition was placed on masters and employers combining but these provisions were enforced with less enthusiasm.

Health and Morals of Apprentices Act 1802

An Act, often seen as the first Factory Act, was sponsored by Sir Robert Peel, amongst his other duties; his family were, ironically, Bury factory owners who employed children. The Act was introduced by Peel, who had become concerned in the issue after a 1784 outbreak of a "malignant fever" at one of his cotton mills, which he later blamed on 'gross mismanagement' by his subordinates

The provisions only applied to pauper apprentices (not those placed by their parents, so-called free children) working in cotton and woollen mills and limited their hours to 12 per day, it also abolished night work and made some provisions for the cleanliness and health of these children.

Textile factories employing 20 or more most have proper ventilation and to be white-washed twice a year. Employers must provide education, decent clothing and accommodation for the children. Enforcement was, again, given to JP's who were empowered to appoint 'visitors'.

The act did provide that in some part of every working day, for the first four years of their apprenticeship, they should be instructed in reading, writing and 'arithmetic', or either of them.

Watch and Ward (Luddites) Act 1812

This was an Act for the more effectual Preservation of the Peace, by enforcing the Duties of Watching and Warding, until the First Day of March 1814, in Places where Disturbances prevail or are apprehended. This Act is in response to the machine-wrecking riots and Acts of violence and murder by the Luddites, especially the attacks on Joseph Foster's mill at Horbury, Wakefield and the Rawfold Mill in Liversedge, both of which occurred in April 1812, as well as disruptions in other parts of the country.

The Destruction of Stocking Frames, etc. (Frame Breaking) Act 1812

The reaction of Parliament to Luddism was to criminalise machine-breaking – the destruction of textile-making machinery – as early as 1721. Initially the punishment was transportation to the Colonies but as a result of continued opposition to mechanisation this Act was passed by the British Government in 1812 aimed at increasing the penalties for Luddite behaviour in order to discourage it. The act made the destruction of mechanised looms – stocking frames – a capital felony (and hence a crime punishable by death). Similarly raised to the level of capital felony were the associated crimes of damaging frames and entering a property with intent to damage a frame. In these respects the act was a stronger version of the 1788 Act, which had made similar acts punishable by 7–14 years transportation. All measures included in the Act were only to be applied temporarily, and were duly set to expire on 1 March 1814.

The Act temporarily allowed judges to administer the death penalty for the crime of damaging frames, citing the "ineffectual" nature of the lesser punishments set out in section four of the 1788 Act. Section four of the 1788 Act was officially repealed by the Capital Punishments, etc. Act 1823, which, whilst not removing the possibility of transportation, gave judges additional room to sentence offenders to alternative punishments such as imprisonment.

Following pressure from various sources, probably including Lord Byron, this Act instituted a new maximum penalty for the destruction of stocking frames of life transportation. In 1817, this Act would itself be repealed and the death penalty once again reinstated in the Destroying Stocking Frames, etc. Act 1817 for a brief period. By this time, however, this particular problem had to a large extent disappeared.

During the period of this Act between 60 and 70 Luddites were hanged!

Importation Act 1815

The 'Corn Laws' were tariffs on imported grain during the early to mid-1800s designed to keep grain prices high to favour producers in Great Britain. The laws did indeed raise food prices and became the focus of opposition from urban groups who had far less political power than rural Britain. The Corn Laws imposed steep import duties, making it too expensive to import grain from abroad, even when food supplies were short. The laws were supported by Conservative landowners, who profited by the law, and opposed by Whig industrialists and workers. The Anti-Corn Law League was responsible for turning public and elite opinion against the laws.

Habeas Corpus Suspension Act 1817

Although mentioned previously, this is a significant suspension of Habeas Corpus in our story. The Home Secretary, Lord Sidmouth, introduced the second reading of the Bill on 24 February 1817. In his speech he said there was *"a traitorous conspiracy...for the purpose of overthrowing...the established government"* and referred to *"a malignant spirit which had brought such disgrace upon the domestic character of the people" and "had long prevailed in the country, but especially since the commencement of the French Revolution". This spirit belittled Britain's victories and exalted the prowess of her enemies and after the war had fomented discontent and encouraged violence: "An organised system has been established in every quarter, under the semblance of demanding parliamentary reform, but many of them, I am convinced, have that specious pretext in their mouths only, but revolution and rebellion in their hearts".*

The Act was renewed later in the parliamentary session. In autumn 1817 Sidmouth went through the list of all those detained under the Act and released as many as possible, personally interviewing most of the prisoners. He also tried to alleviate some of their conditions: "Solitary confinement will not be continued except under special circumstances". The Act was repealed in February 1818 by the Habeas Corpus Suspension Act 1818.[47]

Treason Act 1817

Following on from a stone throwing attack on the Prince Regent this Act made it high treason to assassinate the Prince Regent. It also made permanent the Treason Act 1795, which had been due to expire on the death of George III.

Seditious Meetings Act 1817

This Act was passed by Lord Liverpool's government in March 1817 in retaliation to the March of the Blanketeers from Manchester in the same month. The Act made it illegal to hold a meeting of more than 50 people called "for the purpose...of deliberating upon any grievance, in church or state," unless the meeting had been summoned by an authorised official, or sufficient notice was provided by its organizers. In the latter case, the organizers were required at least five days prior to the meeting to either publicly advertise in a newspaper the time, place and purpose the event, or

---

[47] Wikipedia

submit a notice to a clerk of the peace. The advertisement or notice needed to be signed by seven local persons, and a copy was to be forwarded to a justice of the peace.

The "Six Gagging Acts"

Although enacted after the Pentrich Rising and Thomas Bacon's transportation to Australia, the impact of the Rising and other the numerous challenges to the authority of the government in the period 1812-1817 did provide the stimulus for a series of oppressive pieces of legislation. Although I leap ahead of my timeline, I feel they are worthy of mention.

While these pieces of legislation have been vilified by radical and Marxist historians they were not extreme, given the conditions of the day. The measures were successful in restricting the actions of some extremists and they seem to have been vindicated by the events of the Cato Street Conspiracy in 1820[48].

The Training Prevention Act prohibited civilian bodies from training in the use of weapons. This piece of legislation hardly seems out of place in the modern world, let alone in the period of disaffection of the early 1800's. It also limited the activities of the agent and provocateurs.

The Seizure of Arms Act, linked to the Training Prevention Act, gave JPs and magistrates the right to search private houses for weapons, to seize them and their possessors. This Act also limited the activities of the agent provocateurs.

The Seditious Meetings Act restricted to parish level all public meetings that were called to discuss 'any public grievance or any matter on Church and State'. Organisers had to provide local magistrates with due notice of the time and place of the meeting. The magistrates were empowered to change the date and/or time of the meeting at will, to prevent any attempt to

---

[48] I credit Dr. Marjorie Bloy for her succinct description of the six acts. http://www.historyhome.co.uk

organise insurrection. This was, perhaps, the most serious infringement of public liberty but it was repealed in 1824.

The Blasphemous and Seditious Libels Act fixed the penalties for these activities to fourteen years' transportation. Magistrates were empowered to seek, seize and confiscate all libellous materials in the possession of the accused. This piece of legislation was not especially effective because it was never enforced rigorously, and also because of Fox's 1792 Libel Act. Juries were reluctant to convict people on flimsy evidence.

The Misdemeanours Act provided for speedier legal machinery so that people could be brought to trial faster. This reduced the likelihood of bail being obtained by the accused; it also allowed for quicker convictions. Perhaps this was no bad thing, on either count.

The Newspaper and Stamp Duties Act greatly increased the taxes on printed matter, including newspapers, periodicals and pamphlets. Publishers and printers had to provide securities for their 'good behaviour'. Any publication appearing at least once a month and costing less than 6d was subject to a tax of 4d. The Act restricted the freedom of the legitimate press. Radical publications simply went 'underground'.

13. What about the Women?

I would like to step aside from Thomas Bacon's story for a while to consider the positon of the womenfolk immediately before and at the time of the Pentrich Rising. Although Thomas never married he had a mother and a bevy of sisters to consider and most of the men involved in the Rising would be married, most would be fathers, some grandfathers. We know that the villages of Pentrich, South Wingfield and Swanwick were close-knit and many families were related.

In his influential work on this period Porter[49] tells us that in the eighteenth century 'slightly over half the nation was female. Yet, compared with man, we know little about what working class women felt or thought. Even in upper and middle class homes, it was men who left most records behind – a fact that speaks all too eloquently of how muted women had to be.'

At the end of the eighteenth and in the early years of the nineteenth century it seems unlikely that few if any of the married women of Pentrich, South Wingfield and Swanwick walked to find work at the new factories in Belper or Ambergate; they would normally be home-based.

I must add that we are now, of course, in a very different world when considering the relative position of women in society, their decision-making power and influence some 200 years ago. Whilst I agree with those who would say that, even to-day, we still have some way to go to completely eradicate the 'glass ceiling', establish genuine equality of pay and find more women in the 'corridors of power', it is necessary to concentrate on the period in question.

Probably until the changes brought about by the first world war, it was generally accepted that the role of women was to obey their 'man' (I shrink from use of the word husband in every case), produce and care for as many children as appeared and survived (providing one was male) and to run the household, be it grand or small. In addition, many working class women

---

[49] Porter, Op, Cit.

would be expected to contribute to the household income as best they could. It was also expected that they take care of and support elderly parents. Is it really true that they were no more than drudges and chattels? Certainly pregnant women, those with illegitimate children or with no man on the scene were treated particularly harshly. In an effort to remove them from the support of the parish many were 'found' husbands in other parishes.

Society, the law and the Church supported this position of women at the time and it was seldom challenged in public. However, this said, it is hard to imagine that all the wives and mothers of men associated in whatever degree with the Pentrich Rising never raised an opinion in support or against the proposed actions.

Life in Pentrich, South Wingfield and the surrounding villages was hard and it surely follows that many of the wives and mothers needed to be strong characters merely to survive from one poor harvest or loss of work to the next. Most will have lived through the Luddite activities, in some cases their men would have been directly involved. They would surely have known the severe penalties for involvement in this type of seditious behaviour and, with the number of men involved, it is inconceivable that the women did not know what was being planned in June 1817. The impact on the village of Pentrich was considerable; there was a population of 726 in 1811 and 508 in 1821[50]; many having been forced out by the landlord, the Duke of Devonshire, or the loss of their husband.

Yet, in the original books on the Rising, by Stevens, Neal and White, no mention is made of any objection, contribution or involvement by any women. Is it likely that wives and mothers would allow their menfolk to set off to conquer their 'known world' without serious reservations, specific demands not to go or other obtrusive behaviour – even subtle pressure? Knowing that many may not return and, of critical importance, that their whole financial support structure rested on their husband, father or son.

---

[50] Stevens, Op. Cit. p. 150

Were Derbyshire women so down-trodden as to be unable to express any reservations they must have had? I think not.

We do have some records associated to the widow Nancy Weightman, Thomas' sister, in support of his activities at her pub the White Horse. It is even said that she threatened one of her four sons with a poker when he indicated his reluctance to join the Rising. There are records of Mary Hepworth's bravery in resisting the demands of Jeremiah Brandreth and having her servant killed before her eyes and Mrs Brandreth who made a 'valiant journey' to see her condemned husband in Derby Jail. Other than these, no references exist in the pre-trial period.

It seems that those who suffered the ultimate sanction expressed sympathy but no remorse, for example, in a letter sent by William Turner before his execution he said, ' Dear Father, Mother, Brothers and Sisters, all friends and relations: when it comes to your hand I hope you will compose your minds and spirits and not grieve your departed son. I am perfectly resigned to my fate . . .' Ludlam, another about to lose his head, began a letter 'My dear well belove wife and dear Children . . .'

No remorse, no regrets, no apologies. Are we to conclude that their situation was so bad that they genuinely felt they had no choice and, furthermore, they really believed they would succeed?

I suspect that most of the men joining the Rising, perhaps not those cajoled to do so, took part in protest against their scarcity of work, lack of food, the development of factories taking work from home-based workers and poor treatment by money-grabbing middlemen. In this regard some of the women would have supported their men because they experienced the immediate impact of these issues. But surely there must have been some limit to this support?

Were any questions asked when their men met behind closed doors to discuss their plans? Did they not question the visit by Thomas Bacon and others around the country? What was said on the evening of 9th June when their men and sons left the houses carrying pikes or a firearm? It seems totally inconceivable that they did not know what was planned. It also seems unthinkable that their maternal instincts did not emerge to, at the very least, try to stop what was happening.

Fervently seeking some logic explanation for this apparent benign acceptance to this and without any contemporary records to rely on, it leaves us in the position having, reluctantly, to accept that many were in favour of the actions of their men.

Women and politics was not a concept for general discussion at this time. The idea that women should be given a vote had not emerged as an issue for debate. The suffragette movement demanding votes for women did not begin until 1897 by Millicent Fawcett and then was expanded by Emmeline Pankhurst in 1903.

Arguably the only female radical of the time was Mary Wollstonecraft, 27th April 1759 to 10th September 1797, who was an eighteenth-century English writer, philosopher, and advocate of women's rights. During her brief career, she wrote novels, treatises, a travel narrative, a history of the French Revolution, a conduct book, and a children's book.

Mary wrote her two polemical works, *A Vindication of the Rights of Men* (published anonymously in 1790) and *A Vindication of the Rights of Woman* (1792), both public letters in angry reaction to texts by men whom she considered powerful and wrong-headed. The first answered Edmund's Burke's nostalgic and conservative *Reflections on the Revolution in France*, which argued for the status quo because human nature could not take too much change or reality, and the second responded to Jean-Jacques Rousseau's educational work *Emile*, which proposed that a girl's education should aim at making her useful to and supportive of a rational man.

It would be inconceivable that either of these works ever found their way to the women of rural Derbyshire during the period men were planning the Rising.

Whilst it seems arrogant to ignore half the population in our story, there is no evidence that the women of Pentrich, or South Wingfield ever provided any serious resistance to the Rising. If they did it was no more than words behind closed doors and destined to have little or no effect.

None of the depositions, early books and nothing reported in the trials gives any indication that any women were involved in the march itself. The persuasive influence of Thomas Bacon, Oliver the Spy and others met with little resistance from this source.

Obviously it was a time when the father or husband 'ruled the roost' in most homes and this position was supported, if it became necessary, by contemporary traditions and the law of the land.

However, this said, I find it hard to believe that the wives and mothers had no influence. The existence of a family without a man was harsh indeed, poverty was no picnic, welfare or the provisions for the poor were under the control of the parish and most were not known for their generosity. We are left with the view that many would have remarked, after the disastrous event. *"I told you so!"* But, how many women had said, *"Go with my blessing"*?

14.   1817 Meetings

Arguably the first significant meeting of 1817 was that held at the Crown and Anchor in London on 22nd January, dealt with in chapter ten.

It was in January 1817 and during the process of opening the fifth session of Parliament that the Prince Regent denounced in strong terms the advantages which were at that time being taken of the distressed state of the country, for the purpose of creating a feeling of antipathy. He expressed himself thoroughly determined to use strict means to allay these attempts to disturb the peace of the country which were gradually and surely exciting the masses to acts of violence. There were many who believed that this agitation would die a natural death and amongst this class was the seconder of the address. The Government, it is reported, spent a great deal of time enquiring into the cause of the disturbances and they were found to arise from the distress which prevailed, primarily amongst the lower orders.

When the Prince Regent was returning from the House, some little commotion was caused by an attack made on the carriage in which he was being conveyed and some kind of missile was deliberately hurled though the windows of the conveyance. A message was at once sent from the Lords conveying this intelligence and the House, having decided upon an address to the Regent on this particular incident, shortly afterwards adjourned. Some thought the event to be of a serious nature and that an attempt had been made on the life of the Prince. These suggestions had come from the Ministerial party but, during the resumption of the debate on the following day, the Opposition contended it was no more nor less than an expression of contempt for the Government for the way in which it was said they were discarding the distresses of the people. They also demanded a reduction of expenses and an amendment to that effect was moved.

Lord Sidmouth announced that in the course of a few days the Prince would send down a message bearing on the disaffection of the people, and this message was received on the 3rd of February, ordering certain papers to be laid before the House, respecting the organisations and meetings that were being instituted, not only in the metropolis but in various parts of the country, with a view, it was contended, of disturbing the tranquillity of His Majesty's subjects and to sever, if possible, the affections which had hitherto existed between them and the Government of the realm. The message was referred for consideration to a committee in each House and they reported on the matter on the 18th and 19th of February respectively. The report of the Lords on this matter was to the following effect:-

"The object of the people is, by means of societies or clubs established, or to be established, in many parts of Great Britain under a pretence of Parliamentary reform, to infest the minds of all classes of the community and particularly of those whose situation most expose them to such impressions with a spirit of discontent and disaffection of subordination and contempt of all law, religion and morality; and to hold out to them the plunder of all property as the main object of their efforts and the restoration of their natural rights, and no endeavours are omitted to prepare them to take up arms, on the first signal, for accomplishing their designs."

There would not appear to be much sympathy for the plight of the working class nor, it seems, any efforts to examine their specific claims in any detail.

Nottingham Secret Committee

As we have reported, Thomas Bacon was a regular member of the Nottingham Secret Committee which, allegedly, met almost daily during February, March and April 1817 to keep in touch with similar organisations in other midlands and northern towns[51]. It is reported that Bacon openly discussed insurrection 'with little reserve'. The Secret Committee may well have been a name to replicate the Secret Committees formed by the Government to deal with the Luddites and other 'disturbances', see chapter seven.

---

[51] Neal, op. cit.

Delegates' Meetings

'Delegates' from numerous locations were sent to represent various groups of men in order to report on their activities and co-ordinate progress towards insurrection. For the purpose of attending one of these meetings, Oliver is said to have left London on the 17th of April 1817, in company with Joseph Mitchell who, as delegate from Leeds, had been at the Crown and Anchor meeting in London. They passed through Derby on the 26th and, while coaches were changing, called upon Mr. Robertshaw who was then landlord of the Talbot Inn.

From thence they proceeded to Sheffield and Wakefield, at which latter place a meeting of delegates was held on Monday 5th May 1817, amongst whom was Thomas Bacon who 'appeared to be a very active man among them'. Delegates heard about the plans for Risings in the North and Midlands.

At this meeting, Oliver the 'London delegate' is said to have declared that:

". . . it was in vain to petition Parliament; that all the people in the Metropolis were favourable to a complete change in the Government; that everything was organised and nothing but physical force could effect a revolution; that he was a delegate from London and could, upon a trifling occasion raise a considerable body of men but upon that occasion incalculable numbers to join him in the prosecution of those measures; that it was therefore necessary a general Rising should take place at the same period, and also requisite that all military in every district of the kingdom should be secured in their quarters, their arms seized and the magistrates and other civil officers should be arrested and placed in a state of restraint, not merely that no opposition might be made to the designs of the insurgents but that they might serve as hostages for the safety of such of their own party as might fall into the hands of the Government, and that the men at these meetings ought, without delay, to act upon this project."[52]

---

[52] Neal, op cit.

We get an indication of how Thomas Bacon managed to travel around in a letter sent by Abraham Smith, a 'voluntary informer', to the Home Office[53] in which he describes a meeting at the Nottingham Hampden Club held at the Golden Fleece, Middle Pavement, Nottingham. The letter told of a collection made to send an 'old man', presumably Thomas Bacon, to Manchester to 'see how things were going'. Apparently fourteen shillings and some odd halfpence were collected. Whilst mentioning this letter, it goes on to give an outline of Bacon's influence in that he returned a few days later to report back on communications with the Scotch (sic) Committee.

It is also reported that when Oliver the Spy was engaged on his return to London, doubtless to report to Lord Sidmouth, he stopped off to see Bacon in Nottingham but was unable to do so. It is believed that when Oliver sent his masters the names of delegates to the Wakefield meeting, it was the first time he had mentioned Thomas Bacon who he listed as the Derbyshire, Nottinghamshire and Leicestershire delegate. In this missive he also included comments on William Wolstenholme, a relation of the Rev. Hugh Wolstenholme, 'a brave supporter' of the Derbyshire reformers[54].

After the meeting at Wakefield a second meeting was held on 8th or 9th May, after news of Mitchell's arrest at Huddersfield, according to Neal[55], at a secret and remote house on the Leeds Road. It was at this meeting, attended by Thomas Bacon, William Oliver and other delegates that proposed numbers were gathered. The meeting was eloquently addressed by Oliver, including a poem entitled *The Mother's Last Admonition to her Children!*

Bacon, commenting on Oliver's fashionable appearance said, in his statement made on way to Australia, that the company gave in to Mr Oliver's 'Superior Judgement'. It was agreed at this meeting that the printer of the *Black Dwarf Pamphlet*, Thomas Wooler, would lead the London contingent. It was also agreed that the date of the Rising should be Tuesday

---

[53] HO/42/165, quoted in Neal, op. cit. page 50
[54] Neal, Op. Cit. p.39
[55] Neal, Op. Cit.

27th May 1817. This was the day after Whit Monday and soon after Sir Francis Burdett was to move his Bill for parliamentary reform.

At this meeting Thomas Bacon sold a pair of ribbed hose to William Oliver for 3 shillings and 2 pence from a small stock he of goods he regularly carried with him.

Asherfield Farm Meetings

At 10.00 pm on 17th May 1817, Bacon organised the first of a series of meetings held during the hours of darkness at Asherfield Barn on Sutton's farm, Pentrich, half way between Pentrich and Butterley. They met there with Samuel Haynes, the Leicester delegate. Bacon was the principal orator, passing on the details of the Wakefield meeting. According to Neal[56] he said, ". . . only alternative is to overthrow the government. . ."

At the first meeting at Sutton's Asherfield Barn those present included Armond Booth, a man from Leicester, Thomas Bacon, John Bacon, George Weightman, John Wyld, Joseph Weightman, James Barnes of Swanwick, Edward Haslam of Swanwick and William Smith of Ripley.

According to depositions made by Edward Haslem and Armond Booth, it was at another meeting there 3 or 4 days or a week after when the same persons, with the exception of Thomas Bacon and the Leicester man, attended at this meeting they talked about making pikes procuring arms & gunpowder[57].

Bacon and Butterley Company

It is clear that at some point in mid-May, Bacon began approaching employees of Butterley Ironworks, inquiring about the manufacture of cannon, pikes, firearms and other instruments of war[58]. One such man was

---
[56] Neal, Op. Cit.
[57] Deposition made by A Booth before the trial
[58] Stevens, opacity.

John Cope, a cleaner at the works, who became involved in the Rising. Cope was later to escape punishment by claiming that as the day approached he came to oppose the venture. He told all he knew about Bacon in two statements.

This is corroborated by the depositions, using the words as written:

It was at the 5th meeting at Asherfield Barn about the last day of May or the beginning of June this was a strong meeting, there were present Thomas Bacon (who had just returned from Nottingham) Armond Booth, Michael Onion, John Onion, John Onion Jnr, John Cope, Edward Haslam, Laban Taylor, Joseph & George Weightman, John Wyld, Nathaniel Walters, James Taylor, Isaac Ludlam, William Turner, Coupe, John Hill, William Smith, Burrows, Samuel Walters, John Rodgers and Tapleton alias Stapleton.

The deposition of Armond Booth stated that Thomas Bacon opened the business of the meeting and stated plans of operations which were to commence on Monday night June 9th Depots of arm and ammunition were to be seized and barracks attacked.

It was at the 6th meeting at Asherfield Barn on Thursday June 5th held at 10 o'clock at night which was not quite so numerously attended as the last but consisted of 'nearly the same persons as were present at the former meeting'. A delegate from Leeds who had arrived at Pentrich addressed the meeting exhorting them to be steady, firm and unanimous and assured them that at Birmingham, Leeds, Manchester and elsewhere they were in great forwardness. The Nottingham man (presumably Jeremiah Brandreth) was introduced and explained the plan of operations and the time of Rising was fixed[59].

It was clear that Bacon wanted Butterley employees to join the Rising if for no other reason more than the fact they could gain access to useful material from the factory. Cope gave the opinion that they were too well paid to be

---

[59] Depositions made by A Booth, James Hill, John Storer

interested in revolution. Apparently Bacon replied, *"very well, it did not matter, they would be forced."*

About 2 months since (presumably early April), John Cope stated he was with one Herman (Armond?) Booth and was told Thomas Bacon and his brother was gone to Nottingham to follow 5 London delegates to York.

He, George Weightman brought from old Thomas Bacon as they said and gave to John Cope (who was going to Sheffield) the address of Smith the Landlord of the Blue Bell Sheffield.

Deposition of Armond Booth

The deposition, made after the arrests and before the trials, contains a list of answers to questions **about the activities and travels of Thomas Bacon** mainly during 1817 posed by the solicitor, probably William Lockett of Derby, preparing the prosecution case. **(Clarification, where possible, is included in brackets and in bold)**

A person by the name of Burton came from Nottingham to his house, at Pentrich about the time or very soon after the meeting of delegates in London with petitions for parliamentary reform.

Went with James Barnes to the Queens Head on Alfreton Common where they transacted business with Benbow.

Called a meeting at the White Horse in Pentrich kept by Weightman, which he, Benbow and others attended. **(Probably December 1817 when William Benbow did visit the White Horse Inn)**

Appointed delegate for Pentrich.

Money collected for defraying his expenses to London. About £5 was collected and given him accordingly.

Went to London with petition and in a few days wrote down to Job Walters of Pentrich on the subject of the establishment of a Hampden club. A meeting called in consequence held at his house when his letter was produced & read to the meeting & it was agreed that a Hampden club should be established.

heard him say before he set out for London that he would not give a pin for the petition unless something would come after it. **(Presumed to be the delegates meeting at the Crown and Anchor on 22nd January 1817)**

About Lady Day 1817 **(a religious date – 25th March)** *he stated the number of men enrolled in various parts of the kingdom to overturn the Government were about 400,000.*

A month or 5 weeks before Whitsuntide received a letter from one Stevens of Nottingham supposed to be president of the committee of the Nottingham Hampden club.

Meeting at Ilkeston proposed in consequence of the letter from Stevens.

Met Stevens and Burton (both Nottingham men) 5 or 6 days after at Nottingham.

On his return from Nottingham he set off immediately into Yorkshire or Lancashire for the purpose of forming a plan to overturn the Government and said that he had got some money from Nottinghamshire towards bearing his expenses this was about the 27th April 1817.

Went to Nottingham and other places & has kept going about the country ever since.

Went to one Oliver of Bonsall.

Booth heard him say that he was about to make a second journey into the north & should visit Sheffield, Leeds, Manchester & others in which places it was understood he was commissioned by the Nottingham Committee to visit.

Told Booth & others on his return of his second journey, that it was a bad job that the business he been upon had been put off and understood from him that some appointment had been made for a General Insurrection to take place on Whitsun Monday but that any such insurrection had been postponed.

One John Holmes of Nottingham had also been with him to Sheffield. Went out again and visited Derby, Hinckley, Leicester and other places, & returned by Nottingham.

Said great preparations were making all - over the Empire viz. at Birmingham, Sheffield, Nottingham, Manchester, Leicester, Leeds, London & other places and was informed Scotland was going forward too and all things going on well.

Held meetings again at Pentrich about a month or 5 weeks ago, money collected for Bacons use...

Attended meetings at Asherfield Barn did not attend the second meeting. Opened the business of the 5th meeting so having just returned from Nottingham.

He stated that the country was to use & commence business at the same time, which would be on the Monday night following (9th June) the large towns would rise about midnight and seize all depots of arms & ammunition within their own towns & attack the barracks, etc.

Went to Nottingham on the day after the meeting to acquaint committee that they disapproved of the plan to proceeding to Nottingham immediately and that it would be more advisable to seize upon the Butterley Iron Works.

Was not returned in time for the 6th meeting at Asherfield Barn on the 5th June at 10 o'clock pm but joined before it broke up and brought Jerry Brandreth with him who explained the plan of operations and proceedings.

Was at the meeting at the White Horse in Pentrich on Sunday the 8th June. Sent Joseph Weightman to Nottingham the 8th June by appointment to *know whether the plans still continued unaltered to prevent mistakes.*

A genteel person on horseback came to Pentrich on the 9th before Joseph Weightmans return & reported to the leading men at Pentrich that all things were going on well and that no alteration of plans had taken place.

Deposition of John Cope

The deposition, made after the arrests and before the trials, contains a list of answers to questions **about the activities and travels of Thomas Bacon** mainly during 1817 posed by the solicitor, probably William Lockett of Derby, preparing the prosecution case. **(Clarification, where possible, is included in brackets and in bold)**

About two months **(probably sometime in May 1817)** *ago John Cope met him in Butterley when he said there were delegates going in all parts of the country and there would soon be a general insurrection.*

A few days after this John Bacon told John Cope he was to go to Nottingham to follow six delegates to York.

About ten days after this John Cope met him at Suttons Barn on his return from York, Nottingham & others. Said there was fine work going on & he had to go into Yorkshire again to meet the same delegates and said he must make haste as he expected a general Rising before he could get back. A meeting at the barn of about 20 people it was 11 o'clock at night - Bacon made a speech and said he had been 30 years trying to bring about a revolution and should now succeed.

Told John Cope to do what he could to bring the Butterley people forward who would be forced if they refused.

A day or two before last Whitsunday the Leeds delegate desired George Weightman would inform him that he should send him a letter from Nottingham to let him know how they were going on & whether he (Old Tommy Bacon) was to go to Westminster or not.

On John Copes return from Sheffield he was gone to Manchester.

Met the Leeds delegate, John Cope and George Weightman at the White Horse Pentrich on Friday morning June 6th.

He began to talk of a man of the name of Waine of Nottingham that was to have commanded the people in Derbyshire, but he was ill and the Nottingham man then present was set in his place he and the Nottingham man talked about plans of convention.

Depositions were taken from most of the men who took part in the Rising who were known by the authorities. Much of the material relates to the events on the actual march on the 9th and 10th June 1817 which, of course Thomas Bacon, did not take part in. It is interesting to see, from the reports of meetings during the period up to the Rising, two important points. Firstly, it is clear that Thomas Bacon was one of the leaders of the proposed insurrection and heavily involved in the organisation at a national level. Secondly, at almost every meeting a collection was held to provide funds to support Bacon's travels around the country. I will return to these points in the next chapter.

Change of Date

The date of the Pentrich Rising was originally set for 26th and 27th May to coincide with other similar Risings elsewhere, or so the leaders thought. The date was put off until 9th June – dates which the government were obviously aware off. One reason given for the change was the fact that it would be a new moon and a darker night. Of course, Oliver kept his distance and returned by coach to London on Saturday 7th June.

A variety of reasons have been given including the readiness of other units, particularly those expected in Nottingham, to the prospect of a full moon. The truth may well lie with Oliver's efforts to fit in with his master's plans for troop deployments and to confuse the revolutionaries.

Meeting Dates

Whilst Thomas Bacon spent a great deal of time in the first few months of 1817 travelling around the country from meeting to meeting, some of the precise dates are not recorded. The known dates are:

22nd January - National delegate meeting Crown and Anchor, London
10th March – 'Blanketeers' march set off from Manchester
15th March – A meeting at Spa Fields, London but a handful attended
17th April – Oliver travelled from London
26th April – Oliver in Derby and Nottingham
27th and 28th April Bacon to Yorkshire and Lancashire
3rd May (approx.) – Bacon met Samuel Bamford at Dog & Partridge, Middleton, Manchester at the Hampden Club
5th May – Delegate at Wakefield meeting, Bacon in attendance, William Oliver, 'London delegate' gave a talk
17th May - First of a series of meetings at Asherfield Barn organised by Bacon
23rd May – Thomas Bacon meet William Stevens at Nottingham
26th / 27th May – original Rising dates
31st May - Major planning meeting at Asherfield Barn
2nd June - Bacon visited Stevens at Nottingham
5th June - Meeting at Asherfield Barn, Bacon's last formal meeting
8th June - Meeting at White Horse, led by Brandreth - Bacon absent,

15. London Packet & Lloyd's Evening News 3rd Nov 1817

What the Revolutionaries Wanted

In seeking to understand and illuminate the motivation and declared intentions of Thomas Bacon and his erstwhile colleagues, it may be useful to reproduce yet another perspective. A series of articles entitled the 'The History of the Pentrich Revolution, 1817 – A Derbyshire Insurrection' was written by George Preston JP and appeared in the *Derbyshire Advertiser* at some point after January 1848 when the title came into existence. One particular item, chapter XIV of the series, titled 'An Interesting Addendum' relates to what, it is suggested, the revolutionaries wanted. In other words, what was generally agreed and accepted as the eventual aim of the Rising.

After the publication of the series articles, presumably over a period of weeks, the publishers of the Derbyshire Advertiser received further information from a Belper Resident. The item referred to was a 'preserved' copy of the 'The London Packet and Lloyd's Evening News' dated 3rd November 1817, which contains 'amplified particulars of the ultimate aims of the revolutionaries in attempting to overthrow the King and Government of the country'. In view of the public interest which the history has aroused, and the apparent desire to know every detail relating to it, we subjoin the full extract from the 'Evening Post' as reproduced in the 'Packet and Evening News', of 3rd November 1817.

Following the lead by the *Derbyshire Advertiser*, I will faithfully report the full extract replicating the same phraseology and punctuation. It contains much of the information already known but does go a little further in some respects. When read within the context of our story, it clearly sets out the commanding involvement of Thomas Bacon at every stage up to the 8th June.

The Abstract

The following Statement has appeared in two Ministerial Papers:

Now the State Trials are over, and that the publication of any matters of fact can have no effect on the fate of the parties concerned in the outrages of last June, we proceed to communicate some particulars which did not appear in the course of the examination at Derby, but of the authenticity of which we are well assured.

The meeting of the 8th June was preceded by several others, which paved the way to it. On 17th May, a meeting was held in a barn that stands in the midst of some large fields near Butterley, and which was ordinarily used for the reception of cattle, and indeed appeared fit for no other purpose. Here, on the day above mentioned, Bacon and Samuel Haynes, the Nottingham and Leicester delegates, and many others, attended, and the state of the country was discussed. It was agreed that no redress could be hoped from his Majesty's Ministers and that nothing short of the overthrow of the present Government would do any good. Several exhortations were delivered by the principal speakers (Bacon was one), the object of which was to shew (sic), that the people ought to come forward, and not suffer themselves to be daunted. No particular time was named for the Rising. Cope, a man connected with the conspirators, and who worked at Butterley, was not at this meeting. He had, however, been sent for to the White Horse, at Pentrich, on the preceding night, where he found Bacon, who told him, that he was then going to Huddersfield; and added, they would all be risen in Yorkshire before he came back.

Cannon and Pikes at Butterley

He then inquired about the cannon at Butterley, and wished to know how soon it could be mounted, and whether it would be possible to convey it to Nottingham in two hours. One of the conspirators had said, this might be done, if the best horses in the country were seized to carry it there. To this Cope replied, that it was impossible. Bacon renewed the conversation about the cannon at Butterley, of which he had heard when he was 150 miles off. At Butterley, however, there was in reality but one cannon worth mentioning. This was a four or a six-pounder. Similar smaller pieces were there, which were usually fired on the occasion of any public rejoicing. Cope was further asked, how many cannons could be cast, and how many pikes made a Butterley in a day; and on answering five of the former and 200 of the latter. Bacon said, "That would do – that was plenty." Onion mentioned a place for seizing a depot at Leicester. It was proposed to overpower the garrison by means of sulphur balls. If this failed, the soldier's wives and children were to be seized, and brought up with halters about their necks, and to be put to death if the soldiers refused to surrender.

Nottingham to be the Capital

On the Friday before Whitsunday a man named G. Crabtree, a printer at Bradford, made his appearance at Pentrich. He was then going to South Wingfield, and other places, to inquire what they could do in the cause. This man was the delegate from Leeds, and he occasionally acted a very violent part. The conspirators came to a determination that Nottingham should be made their capital: Birmingham, Manchester and Leeds, were to have local governments provided for them; but Nottingham was to be the principal seat of power. It was proposed to adopt a Constitution founded on that of the United States of America. A convention was in the first instance to sit at Nottingham, to which such county was to be invited to send a member. A Congress was then to be formed, and to sit in the same place, to consider what form of Government ought to be preferred, but the general feeling was, that the constitution of America could not be improved upon.

Whilst making these arrangements, they were not forgetful of the principal appointments necessary to be made in the first instance. Sir F. Burdett they intended to make President; Lord Cochrane was to be placed at the head of the Navy; and Sir R. Wilson they named to be Commander in Chief of the Army. Other Gentlemen, who were known as Reformers, were to be honoured with important appointments.

To secure impartiality on the part of the Generals, it was resolved that no person should have a command in the place where he belonged. Generals were to be sent from Nottingham to Derby, from Derby to York, and vice versa.

A New Bank and a New Coinage

A new bank was to be erected, and a new coinage issued. The Establishment of the Church was to be altogether done away, and the revenues applied to *'better purposes'*.

At one meeting it was taken into consideration what it would be proper to do with members of the Brunswick family who might fall into their hands. It was debated whether it could be better to allow them small annuities to live upon, or whether the proper course would be to put them to death. This discussion was adjourned at the suggestion of old Bacon; who was of the opinion it would be time enough to settle that question when the parties most concerned in the decision should be in their power.

An immense army was to be formed at Nottingham. All the people from Yorkshire, and from the Peak, were to march there, as well as those from Manchester and Birmingham. All the cattle in Leicester were to be seized and brought to Nottingham, for the use of the army.

Several unimportant meetings occurred between the 17th and 30th May; but on the 31st a large meeting took place at Asherfield's barn. Bacon had then just returned from Manchester; he called upon the meeting to appoint a Committee of Arms (a committee to inquire what arms could be procured in the neighbourhood) as it was desirable to know on what they could depend; he said, the time for rising was fixed upon, but it had better not be made public, he wished to distract the attention of Government by frequent alarms, till their friends, like the boy in the fable, should have cried out 'wolf' so often, that the call should be disregarded at last when the wolf actually comes; he said, a Military Committee had been sitting for a fortnight in Nottingham. According to his suggestion, a committee of arms was named, who were to make out lists of arms, and report to the next meeting. It was in consequence of this, that W. Turner produced the South Wingfield estimate at the White Horse, which was read by Ludlam on the 8th June. No other report appears to have been made.

A meeting took place at a private house kept by Brassington. Sentries were placed to guard against surprise. Here, and at Asherfield Barn, it was debated whether, having marched to Nottingham, they should stay there; it was finally determined that this should be decided upon when they were assembled at Nottingham.

Onion, talking on this subject on the evening of the 4th June, endeavoured to forward the interest of the plan, by informing one he met going home that all must go; and it would be better for those who went first, and 'voluntarily'. He had been turned away from the Butterley Works that day, because he refused to withdraw himself from the Hampden Club. He said he did not care. The Revolution would be a better thing for him, as he had no doubt, if they pulled through it well, that he should have no occasion to work anymore.

Brandreth to Command

It was on the 5th of June that Brandreth was introduced to those whom he was to command. Crabtree had returned from Birmingham, where he said all was ready and well, and all the people of Birmingham were so confident of success, that they were quite sure that they could take care of their own soldiers, and not only of their own, but of all the soldiers in England. He exhorted them strongly to go on. The people were only to be firm and unanimous, and they were sure to succeed. Whilst he was speaking, Brandreth came in. He told the meeting they were all to march to Nottingham, to which place he was appointed to conduct them. On the following day Brandreth was introduced to Cope; he inquired if the Butterley men were staunch, as some doubts were entertained of them; he talked about taking the cannon, but this, it was finally settled, should depend on orders from headquarters.

These are the principal incidents in the history of this conspiracy previous to the 8th June. On the 7th the workmen at Butterley were sworn in as Special Constables to defend the works. More than 100 were so sworn in the course of about half an hour. This was a happy thought. Many of them were known to be connected with the conspirators, and when it was heard by their accomplices that they were made Special Constables, the bond of their union was at once dissolved by suspicion. As soon as a considerable number had been seen taking the oath, others, their fellow workmen, animated by l'esprit do corps, of themselves offered to do the same; and these, though known to have been connected with the disaffected, in the hour of severe trial on the morning of 10th June, when Brandreth and his party appeared, conducted themselves remarkably well.

An interested report that I suggest adds a substantial amount to our appreciation of Thomas Bacon's position in the planned Rising. By way of clarification, it must be assumed that the 'Brunswick' family mentioned by Bacon was originally the House of Hanover which was a German royal dynasty which ruled Hanover, and, later, the United Kingdom of Great Britain and Ireland. It succeeded the House of Stuart as Monarchs of Great Britain and Ireland in 1714 and held that office continuously until the death of Queen Victoria in 1901.

16. Tommy Goes Missing

After months if not years of meticulous planning, a succession of secret meetings and a great deal of travelling around the country, the time came for the final push and Thomas Bacon went missing! One could conjure up a variety of potential reasons for his action. Firstly however, it is important to make it clear that we have no evidence of him ever giving an explanation for his conduct in the final days prior to the Rising or immediately afterwards. When, as we shall see later, he 'opened up' on his way to Australia he did not offer any clue to this question.

As with previous aspects of Bacon's life we need to seek facts and corroboration wherever possible. It is an indisputable fact that Bacon was intensely involved in the plans leading up early June 1817. It is a fact that he did not join the marchers at any stage. It is a fact that Thomas Bacon was known to be the leader of the radical movement in and around the Pentrich and South Wingfield area and he was recognised around the country to be so. It was also a fact that he was an old man who walked with a stick and a pronounced stoop. White[60] uses the phrase that 'pertinacious old man' on several occasions.

On 7th or 8th June, the just before the gathering Thomas Bacon took up temporary residence in a hovel owned by James Booth; it was a small single room ram-shackled building secreted in the valley by a track between Pentrich and Buckland Hollow. Throughout his three or four days there, he was provided with victuals by his sister Nanny Weightman of the White Horse. There is no evidence that James Booth knew of Bacon's actions.

According to some reports, he was aware that there was a warrant out for his arrest carrying a reward of 100 guineas. A significant amount of money; depending on which reference you use this is equivalent to over £6,000 at to-day's value. Bacon acknowledges that he knew of the warrant but not when he actually became aware of it. What is also uncertain is **when** the

---

[60] White, Op. Cit.

warrant was issued. If the final arrangements of the Rising, including the revised date, were influenced by William Oliver (the Spy) and known to the authorities, it makes little sense to arrest the man they suspected would be the leader before he set about his treasonous escapade. To do so would leave the prosecution having to prove a conspiracy which, as any lawyer will tell you, is notoriously difficult. Much better to let the Rising start and make the arrest when direct evidence is available – which is, in fact, what happened, but did not include Thomas Bacon! But, are we inferring a level of sophistication that did not exist at the time?

It is a fact that a warrant was in place at some point after the 10th June 1817 when Thomas Bacon and his younger brother John were being sought.

In a statement to his lawyers before the trial he said that a week before the Rising he decided to have *'no more to do with it'*. It is a fact that he made this statement but did he mean it? If he did mean it, why did he change his opinion having been so deeply involved in all the planning? Was it, perhaps, to go some way towards saving his neck?

It maybe that Bacon approached the Nottingham radicals, probably William Stevens, and negotiated a new leader for the Rising, the so-called 'Nottingham Captain' Jeremiah Brandreth. A leader he later introduced to the group at Pentrich on 6th June. It is merely speculation but did he come to the conclusion that he was too old and infirm to take the role of an effective operational commander?

Did he feel that the success of the Rising required a younger, fitter, more determined leader with the necessary charisma to inspire others? Brandreth was considerably younger and did have experience in the Nottingham area.

It has also been suggested that it was the general plan to use leaders from others areas wherever possible. In fact a man by the name of Wain of Nottingham was designated to lead the Pentrich Rising but became ill and was replaced by Brandreth. This may well have been the case but it does not adequately explain Bacon's decision to go into hiding.

Bacon had been an integral part of the detailed planning process for around a year and was regularly to be seen at meeting around the midlands, north and even London. Was it not a strange time to remove himself from the Rising? Was it simply a loss of nerve? He knew, of course, that he would be a key target for those making the arrests.

There is evidence, set out elsewhere, to verify the fact that he had been approaching employees of Butterley Company in May, particularly John Cope, seeking various arms, metal devices to unseat horse riders and even cannons. In his deposition, John Cope describes how Thomas Bacon sought to gain access to cannons, pikes and other metal work from Butterley Company. This is clear evidence of his involvement but, not necessarily of his intention to join the Rising.

It has also been suggested that he finally developed an intense suspicion of William Oliver, the spy, and decided the march was doomed. There is some corroboration in that the Nottingham group were developed serious doubts against William Oliver's role and status. Did Bacon warn any of his friends? Did he warn Jeremiah Brandreth and, if he did would he have taken heed? It seems to be accepted that Brandreth and Oliver did not meet, but did he know of his existence and the extent to which he had latterly been involved?

A similar scenario had taken place in Huddersfield a few days previously when arrests were made and the involvement of William Oliver was well known. It seems that no-one in the Derbyshire - Nottinghamshire area knew of this and, of course, we must remember that communications between locations sixty miles apart was far from instantaneous.

The case has been made that Thomas Bacon was a well-respected leader and had been so for some time. If he had taken steps to warn others, is it not likely his advice would have been heeded? Is this sufficient logic to assume that Bacon did not warn others? It seems illogical that Bacon should remove himself from the Rising because of his suspicions about Oliver and yet not take more positive action to dissuade his friends and family members from embarking on the doomed episode.

At 64 years he was the oldest of the potential revolutionaries and the walk to Nottingham, not to mention the plans to continue walking to Newark and then London, may have not been to his liking or even his capabilities. It was known that he walked with the aid of a stick and had a pronounced stoop. Would he have been more of a liability than an asset?

Most writers suggest that Brandreth, somewhat late on the Pentrich scene, was intent to move whatever. None of the depositions or any aspects of the trial evidence suggest that Bacon attempted to stop others from Rising. Perhaps he never intended to take part at all?

Thomas Bacon's decision to absent himself on the eve of the Rising is one of the most debated and interesting elements of this story. He was a dedicated republican, he believed in the radical dream and he, without doubt, was no fool. Why did his sister Nancy provide him with food when she had been a staunch supporter of the cause for many years? Who else knew of his decision and his whereabouts? How did the other leaders, Weightman, Turner and the rest, react to his absence? As we shall discover later, there were considerable efforts made by the crown lawyers to keep him out of the witness box when many questions may have been answered.

Finally, there is an alternative interpretation. If it is assumed that a warrant was in existence before the Rising, he could have been arrested at any stage – the bounty could well have tempted someone! Perhaps he realised that he could be arrested at any time and subjected to what can only be termed 'aggressive questioning' leading to the revelation of the plans and details of the Rising. His decision to keep out of the way may, perhaps, have removed that particular risk.

Thomis[61] offered the explanation 'it was possible that Bacon's growing apprehension that successful revolution might involve action as well as words that caused his enthusiasm to cool in the later stages of the conspiracy, a coolness that was to lead to his eventual defection from the cause. Perhaps Bacon was essentially a man of words, not action . . .'

---

[61] Thomis, Op. Cit.

Bacon had been to Nottingham and brought Jeremiah Brandreth back to Pentrich; why would he do this if he anticipated disaster? Was he giving the Rising a better chance of success by delivering a younger, more capable leader or was he merely 'pretending' to do so?

Was he saving his head or is that just too ridiculous given his involvement over the years?

On this particular aspect of the story the scenario poses many more questions than answers. It offers many different explanations which, it appears, we are never going to clarify one way or the other. It is left with you, dear reader, to weigh up the few facts we do have, the circumstances set before you and the feasibility of the various explanations.

17.   The Rising

Despite a rescheduling of the date and a late change of 'general', the gathering took place on the evening of Monday 9th June 1817. Jeremiah *The Nottingham Captain'* Brandreth and George Weightman meet the first group at Hunt's Barn, South Wingfield. Doubtless some would have made comment about their missing leader Thomas Bacon; a man who had been recognised as the 'heart and soul of the entire event'. Bacon was undoubtedly the key driver, planner and motivator over the recent months and, probably, years. However, Brandreth who took over the leadership with confidence and enthusiasm was nothing if not determined and this imparted a degree of confidence to the group. If questions were raised about Bacon they were not recorded or reported. It is impossible to conceive that no-one asked where Owd Tommy was

On a wet miserable night they set out through the rain, mud and dark lanes some fixed on changing the government, others because they were pressurised in to joining and some for the excitement. They had been told that similar armed groups would be setting off from Manchester, Nottingham, Derby, Huddersfield and even in London itself. The first meeting of groups were to be at Nottingham, then by boat to Newark and thereafter to meet the assembled masses in London. Whether the change of date had been communicated to the other locations is unknown, but unlikely. It is recorded that a small group did begin to move in Huddersfield but did not get very far; most of the other groups did not even set off!

Their intention in the early stages was for two or perhaps three separate groups to call at every dwelling where they knew, from their previous survey, firearms could be obtained. Several small groups joined as the Rising progressed around the area, from Ripley, Alfreton and a few from Heanor. Visits to some dwellings yielded both men and weapons whilst others were strongly resisted. Brandreth was aggressive and threatening, several men were 'pressed' into joining at the point of a gun. It was noted that any who were 'pressed' into joining were not allowed to carry a firearm, even if they provided one – the firearms were carried by the 'trusted' lieutenants.

With the rain, darkness and muddy farm tracks, it must have been an exhausting trek moving from dwelling to dwelling.

Prior to the actual day of the Rising, there had been talk of 'drawing the badger' and by this they intended to draw out the local magistrate Colonel William Halton and murder him. However, he had been warned of the Rising and waited with his gun and a few retainers at South Wingfield – the marchers never arrived. There were many more 'visits' and a few more men enlisted; some pikes, scythes and a few firearms were commandeered.

The Death of Robert Walker

The group led by Brandreth, some 30 or 40 men, found their way to Mrs Mary Hepworth's farm in Wingfield Park. Brandreth and Daniel Hunt attempted to gain access to the house in order to find recruits for the march and any firearms they suspected might be in the farmhouse. They eventually forced entry via some loose shutters to encounter Mrs Hepworth, a widow, her daughter, one of her sons and two servants. One of the servants was called Robert Walters. Brandreth demanded weapons and her menfolk to join the Rising. For a reason not entirely clear, Brandreth noticed a movement and fired into the kitchen. The bullet struck Robert Walters who was stooping down to lace his boots. He was killed on the spot. Some said Walters was even preparing to join the march. Nevertheless, murder had been committed and this aroused several of the group who remonstrated with Brandreth. He replied that it was his duty to do so and threatened to shoot them also for their insolence.

This incident doubtless served to be an encouragement to the more committed marchers and, at the same time, the source of intense trepidation to those harbouring reservations about the whole affair.

They left Mrs Hepworth with her family and the body. They progressed towards Pentrich where they met another group who had been working their way towards them. It will never be known what impact the killing had on the other groups they encountered; did it create excitement or fear?

After being joined by other small groups and making several other 'visits', the marchers were assembled in military file in two lines and marched towards the next stage in their plan, that being to access weapons and men from Butterley Company located between Swanwick and Ripley.

Mr Goodwin and Butterley Company

The plan was to take possession of Butterley Ironworks and take whatever would be useful. However, if there had been any doubt that the secrecy of the Rising had been breached it would be obvious here. There had been a large number of recently sworn-in special constables posted under the direction of the works manager, the indefatigable George Goodwin. They kept watch all night and reportedly heard guns shots and other noises in the surrounding area. It was not until three or four in the morning that the 100 or so matchers appeared through the rain. By this time many of the special constables had been stood down. The bravery of Mr Goodwin was evident when he faced Brandreth and told him he would have none of his men and none of the ironworks. He and the remaining special constables were faced by a much larger force but his resistance was resolute and successful. Maybe they did not relish the fight; maybe the killing had squashed the enthusiasm of some. Of course, Goodwin did know many of the marchers personally and was able to challenge them by name.

The stubborn resistance had two immediate effects, firstly, it took Brandreth by surprise – he evidently had not expected to be refused in his demands. Despite being armed and supported by a superior force he was set back on his heels. Secondly, the rebuke from Mr Goodwin must have had an impact on the marchers who, wet and bedraggled, could see a flaw in their leader. It is fair to add that Butterley Company was known to be a good employer in the area and the matchers would not have been keen to follow up Brandreth's demands with direct force.

There was further evidence of Mr Goodwin's determination when he stopped William Weightman who was passing by on horse-back and carrying a large bag secreted under his smock. Mr Goodwin grabbed the horses bridle, and seized the bag which, it transpired, contained some 84 lbs of bullets. Obviously, he was a man not to be trifled with!

Onwards and Upwards

The marchers set off to Ripley, doubtless with low spirits and wet backs, where they met up with a few other groups emerging from different directions. It was from this point that some of the group took the opportunity to sneak away.

Undeterred, Brandreth raised three cheers and set the group matching towards Codnor where they stopped to take bread and ale at the Glasshouse Inn, New Inn and French Horn public houses.

Despite appointing trusted lieutenants front and rear some of the marchers, particularly those 'pressed into service against their will' took their chance to escape through the mist and rain. In actual fact Brandreth did have several confrontations with marchers attempting to leave the gathering; despite threats to shoot them he did not take any such action.

Brandreth needed to find out what was happening elsewhere. Looking back some 200 years, it is difficult to imagine how one would get an urgent message from one location to another. The only option to the Pentrich marchers would have been for someone to mount a horse and take it there! A little later, George Weightman commandeered a pony and did set off with an instruction from Brandreth to ascertain 'the state of play' in Nottingham. When he returned the main group were approaching Langley Mill. Weightman and Brandreth held a private conversation, the outcome of which was not relayed to the others. It was suggested by Neal that the report was not favourable and a more positive spin was passed to the troops which seemed to have a degree of encouragement. One can only imagine the mental conflict in the minds of Brandreth and Weightman.

Towards the End

On arriving at Eastwood they saw many residents out of their houses to observe the Rising; how did they know? After further refreshments at the Sun Inn they set off towards Nottingham. By this time there were probably less than 150 of the original group, estimated to have been almost 400 men at one stage.

The end came swiftly as they approached Giltbrook, close to where the 'Ikea' store is now located, where they met a small detachment of the 15th Hussars under the command of Captain Phillips accompanied by a magistrate Launcelot Rolleston. If any doubts still existed as to the authority's knowledge of the march they were removed here. The marchers scattered in all directions leaving their pikes and rifles lying in the road. There was no attempt to engage in any resistance with the troops despite the marchers' superior numbers. It had been often said in the various meetings that the troops were supportive of the insurrection and would refuse to leave their barracks to deal with the Rising. This did not prove to be the case.

Between 50 and 60 were detained and 40 pikes and guns collected by the troops. Many of those who had fled, including Jeremiah Brandreth, were arrested during the next few days. Of course, neither Thomas Bacon nor William Oliver was anywhere to be seen!

The Pentrich Rising was at an end. The work of Oliver the Spy had been successful. The Rising had been totally squashed and, it must be said, by a small force of Hussars.

The question remains as to how many of the marchers really thought they would reach Nottingham, progress on to London, succeed in over-running the government and achieve a significant change in their miserable existence. However, the arrests and heavy punishment doled out to some did make a major and enduring difference to their future and that of their families left behind in Pentrich and South Wingfield.

Are men so easily led?

An afterthought at this stage is to consider when and how Thomas Bacon received the news of the total disaster of the Rising that he had been so dedicated to. Did he really think the authorities would be satisfied with those they had arrested and forget about Owd Tommy?

18. The Huddersfield Story

Members of The Huddersfield Local History Society have completed an extended review of all the events in their area leading to an uprising to coincide with plans elsewhere, including those in Pentrich. The resulting document contains a great deal of specific detail including names and places. Those with a particular interest in these events will find the effort of obtaining and reading this document well worth it. With the permission of the group, I include a few abstracts from their excellent research document. My intention is to give an insight into, on the one hand, the fact that the Pentrich Rising was not an event unconnected with similar activities elsewhere and, on the other, provide further evidence of involvement of Thomas Bacon on a wider scale. Where explanations are necessary or relevant details useful I include them in brackets.

Readers seeking further information about the events in Huddersfield are recommended to refer to the source I make reference to below[62].

Although organisation existed within the West Riding, and probably with adjacent manufacturing districts, there is no evidence of direct links with London other than through (Joseph) Mitchell, which accords with (Samuel) Bamford's account of his role and (William) Oliver's appraisal of him as the 'principal agent of communication.' How well Mitchell was known in the Huddersfield area before this time is not known. He certainly had a contact in the district since, on the 4th May (1817), returning from Liverpool for a delegate meeting at Wakefield, he got off the coach near Huddersfield to visit someone. Consequently, from now on, liaison between the different manufacturing districts was mainly carried out by 'the London delegate, Mr Oliver.'

The major meeting, for which Mitchell was returning, went ahead in his absence at Wakefield the next day (5th May 1817). Tom Bacon, a veteran

---

[62] "Death or Liberty – The Road to Folly Hall 1813-1817" by Huddersfield Local History Society
http://www.huddersfieldhistory.org.uk/huddersfields-history/

Republican and Luddite suspect, from Pentrich in Derbyshire, was present, fresh from a meeting with Bamford at Middleton. Sheffield was represented by William Wolstenholme (a relation of the Pentrich curate Hugh Wolstenholme) and others. There were delegates from Birmingham, Leeds, Barnsley and Huddersfield. Vastly inflated reports were given of the radicals' strength in the respective districts – (it was) said they could raise 8,000 men in the Huddersfield area.

... at a Sheffield meeting, whether because of apprehension about the state of preparedness among local leaders, or due to a wrecking tactic by Oliver, it was suddenly decided to postpone the rising from Whit Monday, the 26th May, until the 9th June, ostensibly to avoid a night of the full moon.

Although this plan may have emanated from Oliver it was similar to the tactics proposed elsewhere. In Huddersfield, a plan to raid Milnsbridge House and take the 30 stand of arms stored there.

Thus well-armed and with the magistrates and other main opponents captured, the revolutionaries expected to surround and disarm the military garrisons with little resistance. Although Oliver may have misled the Radicals over the level of support to be expected from London, he cannot be blamed for fostering delusions about local strength. Nor can the details of preparations be traced to him. None of the schemes which came to light would have stretched the imagination of local revolutionaries – (some) had been dreaming up plans for at least five years. Even if Oliver had never appeared on the scene the rising would have gone ahead, since the Radicals had wildly optimistic views of the revolutionary mood of the people. The fact that some persisted with the scheme, even after it became evident things had gone terribly wrong, testifies to this misjudgement.

Ten delegates were arrested and escorted into Wakefield by a troop of Yeoman Cavalry, who were stoned, while an 'immense assemblage' gathered around the Court House, indicative of the strong popular sympathy which the revolutionaries hoped to tap.

Over the following weeks numerous arrests were made in the rebel areas. A detachment of the 13th Dragoons was stationed in Huddersfield to assist the Yeomanry and 130 men of the 33rd Regiment of Foot in rounding up suspects and searching for arms. Fears persisted that the insurgents were planning another attempt, and signal shots and beacons on the hills were reported. About 30 men were held for questioning and then taken under cavalry escort to York Castle.

The Leeds Mercury had investigated the role of Oliver and condemned the way he, as a government agent, had actually encouraged the revolutionaries by false assurances of support in London. By the time of the York Summer Assizes there was widespread sympathy among even middle class parliamentary reformers for 'Oliver's dupes.' Few of the insurgents turned King's evidence.

Besides the reliability of the prosecution witnesses being challenged a number of respectable character witnesses spoke for the defendants. Fortunately, the political climate had changed since 1812 and hostility to the government outweighed fears of revolution among many of the middle classes. After only a quarter of an hour the jury returned the verdict of not guilty. With a stern warning from the judge about their narrow escape the men promised to watch their future conduct. The esteem in which the liberated men were held was shown on the 27th July when they were met on their approach to Huddersfield by an immense number of men, women and children who hailed their safe return. The scenes which were exhibited between the men and their families and the boys and their parents at this happy meeting we shall not pretend to describe.

Their Derbyshire counterparts were less fortunate - three were hanged and 14 transported for from 14 years to life. The Yorkshire trials also had their tragic sequel. Riley, still in York castle in October, cut his own throat, leaving a widow and ten children. Lee was left to help clean up the suicide cell. He was released at the end of the year, as was Whiteley, just before the Habeas Corpus Suspension Act expired, the government preferring to let the embarrassing episode drop.

The 1817 uprising reveals a high degree of amateurism and self-deception amongst the insurgents, but they cannot be dismissed as mere dupes of Oliver. There was a belief widespread among working people that an armed uprising, a march on London and the overthrow of the government would establish a democratic political system and economic improvement. Exactly what form this would take may not have been clear to all the participants, although some certainly wanted a Republic. Supporters of the ideas of Thomas Spence desired fundamental economic change, involving the break up and distribution of the great aristocratic landholdings, but it is unclear how established the Spenceans were outside London. Mitchell subscribed to their views two years later and may have been propagating them in 1817. Resistance to the further spread of industrialism was undoubtedly one of the unspoken objectives of the rising and it is clear from the numerous references to Luddism that many of the rebels of 1817 considered they were carrying on where those of 1812 had left off. Similarly, the experiences of 1817 were taken into account in the preparation of the next rising, after legal outlets of popular protest had again been blocked.

19. The Trials

Pre-Trial Processes

The pattern followed during the trials does indicate the ultimate objectives of the government in terms of who was prosecuted and for what offence. There were anomalies in that some were prosecuted for relatively minor involvement and others released or not proceedings against after undertaking a more significant role.

When writing about the trial arrangements, William Lockett, the Derby Solicitor in charge of the prosecution, expressed a wish that the opening should be delayed until after the harvest period. This particular point gathers more significance when one finds that the vast majority of jurors were farmers; there were none who could be termed as 'peers' of the prisoners – there no stockingers, no labourers, no miners!

Lockett also made some suggestions about how the proceedings were to be organised in that the prosecution of eight or ten for High Treason would be considered sufficient to set an example, which, it seems, was the main objective. On the latter point the Home Office took a more aggressive line suggesting as many of the insurgents who rose on 10th June as can be fixed by the evidence should face High Treason. However, Lockett's main source of anxiety was that Thomas Bacon was, at that stage, still at large despite the fact that a 100 guineas reward was offered for his capture. The fact that the reward was mentioned at this stage would seem to corroborate the scenario that the arrest warrant and reward were issued after the Rising and not before the event as has been suggested by some, see chapter sixteen.

Lockett did not have to wait long however, as Thomas and his brother John were arrested at St Ives, Huntingdon on 15th August after a struggle[63]. Apparently they did not surrender graciously and a local constable was given 'a severe blow with a bludgeon'.

---

[63] HO/42/169; *Cambridge Chronicle and* Journal, 22nd August 1817, Neal, Op. Cit. p79

Neal reports that when the Bacons were taken to Derby Jail. Shortly after their incarceration a magistrate expressed concern worried about Tommy's attitude.

"I conclude you are aware," he wrote to the Home Office early in September, *"that that old scoundrel Thomas Bacon evidently intends to plead his having been a dupe to Oliver. . . This is pretty well of a fellow that had declared he had been thirty years endeavouring to stir up this insurrection."*

It is quite clear that the authorities knew a great deal about Thomas Bacon and his antecedents. It also reinforces the fact that the 'removal' of Tommy was a key element of their strategy.

The report on the Proceedings opened with the following comments;

A number of misguided and illiterate men, having in company with others, assembled together in the neighbourhood of Alfreton, in the County of Derby, and with arms in their hands, attempted to march through the county to the town of Nottingham, they were, on the 10th June 1917, by the activity of the magistracy, aided by the military power, apprehended, and lodged in the prisons of Derby and Nottingham. Shortly after, a Special Commission passed the great seal, for the trial of these unhappy individuals, in the county hall of Derby, on a charge of High Treason.

In consequence of this, happily, very unusual occurrence, preparations were made accordingly, and the county hall was entirely altered for the occasion, and court laid out in such a manner, as to afford the greatest possible accommodation to the company which was expected to attend on so solemn an occasion.

High Treason is the crime of disloyalty to the Crown. Offences constituting high treason include plotting the murder of the sovereign; committing adultery with the sovereign's consort, with the sovereign's eldest unmarried daughter, or with the wife of the heir to the throne; levying war against the sovereign and adhering to the sovereign's enemies, giving them aid or comfort; and attempting to undermine the lawfully established line of succession.

Considered to be the most serious of criminal offences, high treason was often met with extraordinary punishment, because it threatened the security of the state. Hanging, drawing and quartering was often employed. The last treason trial was that of William Joyce, better known as 'Lord Haw Haw', who was executed in 1946 – but not beheaded, drawn and quartered.

The first day of the trials was set as Wednesday 15th October 1817. The report on the proceedings continues that:

On Tuesday evening, the town of Derby began to be thronged with strangers, and it is worth notice, that the prisoners are, most of them, in the lowest situation in life, men without property and without influence, only one of them being, in dress and appearance, a wit above the situation of a working mechanic or labouring man[64]. Some of them appeared in Court with smock-frocks, and others evinced by the clothing, that they were the sons of poverty. Notwithstanding this, their trials have excited extraordinary interest and attention, not only in the town of Derby, but in the neighbouring counties, and indeed, throughout the whole kingdom, so that the town is crowded with company in an unprecedented manner.

The final stage of the pre-trial exchanges was an announcement by the Chief Baron, Sir Richard Richards:

"I wish the gentlemen present to be informed that it is the expectation of the Court that no part whatsoever of the proceedings to begin tomorrow, will be in any way published, till the whole shall be concluded. I state this with the full concurrence of the Court, that it may be known it is their determination to take due notice of any publication that may take place, if this notice should not be attended to."

---

[64] This is believed to have been Samuel Hunt

The Trials Begin

It is interesting to note that the first name on each count listed on the indictment was, even before Brandreth, Weightman and Turner, that of Thomas Bacon, late of the parish of Pentridge (Pentrich), labourer.

This said the trials proceeded in logical sequence with those against whom the strongest and conclusive evidence existed. The trial of Jeremiah Brandreth began on Thursday 16th October, William Turner on Monday 20th October, Isaac Ludlam, the elder, Wednesday 22nd October and of George Weightman on Friday 24th October; all four pleaded not guilty. Numerous witnesses were produced, questioned and cross-examined, addresses were made to the jury of farmers and each, in turn and with the minimum of deliberation, was found guilty of High Treason. The variation in this was that, after returning a 'guilty' verdict in the case against George Weightman, the jury asked the judge to exercise a degree of mercy.

The Sentencing

The proceedings concluded with sentencing on Saturday 25th October 1817. The first contingent to be arraigned before the court was Thomas Bacon, his brother John Bacon and seven others were arraigned before the Chief Baron, Sir Richard Richards. Mr Denham, Counsel for the defence, requested that the court allow the prisoners to withdraw their original pleas of 'not guilty' and to plead 'guilty' to the charge against them. The charge was read again and all duly entered pleas of 'guilty'. Doubtless some discussions had been held elsewhere of which we have no record. One could only imagine the nature of the 'plea-bargaining' with Thomas Bacon – a choice between the hangman's noose and a trip to Australia.

During the trial, Bacon was described as a man of 'rude and uncultured' appearance yet possessing 'an excellent natural understanding, a degree of knowledge far beyond the attainment of men of his condition of life and a most artful and insidious manner'.

At this point Bacon was a silver-haired man of middle height, with a yellow-complexion, his face pitted with pock marks. His had silver locks to his shoulders and 'had the need of a walking stick'. He walked in a distinctive stooping manner. In the context of the times at 64, he was an old man.

Goodwin, the Butterley Company manager was heard to say, "(Thomas Bacon) . . . was the ring-leader and mover of the plot and deserved hanging most richly . . . Thomas Bacon was a rascal."

After the first group, containing the Bacon brothers, a further twelve were arraigned before the judge. This group contained Isaac Ludlam's brother, and amongst the others there were three Weightmans. The prosecution informed the judge that they were to offer no evidence against this group and, accordingly, they were formally dismissed and released with a severe warning from the Chief Baron relating to their future conduct.

In the last group to be brought in chains before the court were Jeremiah Brandreth, Isaac Ludlam, the elder, William Turner and George Weightman. The Lord Chief Justice adopted a solemn manner and the 'black cap' was placed on his head. After a long address he ended with these words:

"I . . . must pass upon you the awful sentence of the law; which is, that you and each of you must be drawn on a hurdle to the place of execution, and there severally hanged by the neck until you are dead; your heads must then be severed from your bodies, which are to be divided into four quarters, and to be at his Majesty's disposal."

This was the traditional sentence for any person convicted of high treason and had been so far centuries.

After the sentencing of the four principals, the judge handed down various sentences including that Thomas Bacon and his brother John Bacon were to be transported for life.

On Sunday 2nd November, 1817, the warrant arrived confirming the death sentence on Brandreth, Turner and Ludlam; the execution was set for Friday 7th November. A decision on George Weightman was postponed for a week; thereafter he was kept separate from the three facing the ultimate sanction. The warrant confirming the death sentence, signed by Lord Sidmouth on behalf of the Prince Regent, did in fact change the originally sentence marginally. The hanging and beheading was confirmed but the quartering was remitted!

Two days after the executions, George Weightman, who was Nancy Weightman's son, was given the news of his reprieve; his sentence was down-graded to transportation for life. The clemency allowed to George was because of his age, around 25, and the fact that he was not active on the march being 'a kind of despatch rider between Pentrich and Nottingham'.

Bacon's Guilty Plea

The evidence against Thomas Bacon was never put before the jury due to his change of plea to one of guilty. There is a strong argument that, if Bacon had been tried, the prosecution would have had some difficulty in proving the offence on the indictment.

The first count of High Treason would have required evidence that Thomas Bacon 'waged war against the King, arming himself, and marching through the countryside in hostile array'. He clearly did not do this as he disappeared before the match began.

The second element of High Treason, a lesser indictment, would have required evidence that Bacon had . . . 'meeting to devise, arrange and mature plans and measures to subvert and destroy the Constitution.' The prosecution were using the meeting on 8th June 1817 to provide this evidence but, as we have outlined, Thomas Bacon removed himself before this event. Apparently John Cope and Armond Booth were willing to testify on this second point but were sure to be discredited.

Did Bacon realise this? Did his counsel advise him accordingly? Obviously the prosecution were under instructions to avoid producing Oliver the spy or even having his name brought into the trial and Bacon would certainly have done this had he been given the opportunity.

Did they exchange a 'guilty' plea in a guarantee of a non-capital sentence or, as Thomis[65] intriguingly suggests '. . . Thomas Bacon's freedom was the price paid for the lives of his fellow-prisoners, a not ignoble fate for him to suffer. . . whether his lawyers ever explained this situation to him is not known.'

It is quite obvious that the authorities were intent on removing Bacon from his position as the radical influence in the region. If not by severing his head then by placing him out of sight and mind several thousand miles away; an acceptable alternative.

---

[65] Thomis, Op. Cit.

20. After the Trial

It was commented on by one of the jailers that Bacon was 'stirring up' the prisoners even after their sentence by telling (the prisoners) that they are not tried by their peers but men of property, a jury consisting wholly of farmers. He was further quoted as saying, *"I name this to show what dreadful principles these men have taught their unfortunate children."* Of course, in this regard Bacon was correct, the Grand Jury was made up of the 'great and the good' of Derbyshire and the trial juries hearing the evidence in the various trials were farmers - 'men of property'.

It seems Thomas Bacon was not the most popular prisoner, the Chaplain of Derby Jail noted that when Brandreth, Turner and Ludlam were together in the condemned cell, they blamed Thomas Bacon for their situation. In particular, Turner expressed dissatisfaction with his trial and suggested many witnesses were lying; he also blamed Thomas Bacon's 'artful devices' for his downfall. This may be one of the criticisms set against Bacon's behaviour in absenting himself from the Rising or, maybe, it goes much deeper than that.

The chaplain reported that Ludlam, who had been a Methodist lay preacher, was 'truly and sincerely penitent, never blaming Oliver at any time but accusing Brandreth and Bacon of the chief part in fermenting the sedition.

On 28th November 1817, Thomas Bacon and nine of his co-prisoners were transported from the Derby County Jail to Newgate Prison in London. On 30th November they were moved to the prison hulk *'Retribution'*, moored at Sheerness, to await embarkation.

Mr Eaton, the Derby Jailer, took the ten prisoners of the first party down to the hulk at the mouth of the River Medway, and recorded an interesting conversation with Thomas Bacon in a letter to the Home Office[66]:

---

[66] HO/40/7 (8PT 1) quoted by Neal, Op. Cit.

"... whilst on the road with the convicts to Sheerness Thomas Bacon told me that he believed he could give more information to Government than any other Man – he likewise informed me that Brandreth would not have commanded the Party tha Night had not a Person, I think the Name of Rochefort been very ill upon TB giving the Name of this Man he was immediately called to order by his brother John Bacon- he likewise informed me of another Plan that had been strongly recommended by a man of the name of Grovenor (Gravener) Henson which was to take possession of all the principal Estates a Plan was produced on which Roads to the different Points was drawn in Lines of different colours . . . This plan TB says he opposed as not likely to answer . . ."

One week before Christmas 1817, Bacon and the others were placed aboard the '*Tottenham*', a sail ship of 557 tons bound for Australia. Their situation did not improve by the fact that, due to storm damage, they did not set sail for another four months, until 17th April 1818. They arrived in Sydney harbour on 14th October 1818. There were 200 prisoners and crew on board together with 34 soldiers. Ten prisoners died on route but none of the Derbyshire contingent although many were ill.

When one considers the length of the voyage and the conditions in which prisoners were commonly detained it speaks highly of the firm constitution and strength of character of Thomas Bacon, approaching the age of 65. The time spent on the ship before sailing and the journey itself would severely test the constitution of any man.

Stevens[67] records that once aboard the *Tottenham*, Bacon made a further statement. He told of his suspicions of Oliver in early June, how he told Stevens (William Stevens, Nottingham radical and needle maker) the scheme should be dropped and how Stevens *'put himself in a Wrath and said did not Mr Oliver and the London Gentleman know best what to do?'* Stevens, said Bacon, assured him that *'he could put his life on Mr Oliver's hands.'* Four days before the Rising, said Bacon, he went to Nottingham

---

[67] Stevens, Op. Cit.

and told Stevens he was having nothing more to do with the Rising. Stevens *'then sent for a man that came with me in to Derbyshire he was a stranger to me and I did not know his name til I was in prison which was Brandrif that shot the man.'*

Bacon claimed that he saw William Turner at some of the meetings, but he never heard anything violent from Turner. Ludlam he never saw at a meeting, and did not know he had anything to do with it until he saw him in prison.

'When I was first in prison, some magistrates came I offerd to tel [them of] the affair but Mr Locket The pricicutor Discharged me from speaking one word I was the first man in the indictment it was King against Thomas Bacon and others, My trial was copoo'd to Come on the First . . . I never heard till the Special sizes that the man had comit'd such violence for that was not the meaning of the affair on the principle of what is called Universal Suffrage & Annual Parliaments, It is manifest Oliver over Acted his part by Exciting if instead of Detecting it But If it had not been for publick Distress it would have been In vain for Mr Oliver to [have] excited the Disturbance.'

Bacon then turned to the prisoners aboard the *Tottenham* with him:

'Hill & Bettison I never Knew until I was in prison Also Manchester Turner, Josiah Godber, German Buxton, George Brassington & John Mackisswick nor did I know they had any Concern George Weightman it is manifest there was a Great Deal more said than what was true As to John Bacon the pricitter Lockett said he had not much against him for He had Inqured into his carrector and found hit was A very Good one. And George Weightman the same.'

Bacon complained that the prisoners felt they had been harshly treated compared with the Yorkshire (Huddersfield and Sheffield) rioters who had been sent home to their families, and added: *'it has been held out by Christians that one offence In their passage through Life ought to be forgiven, and we hope that our past & future conduct Will Regain us a medigation of our severe sentence.'* Bacon then thanked Lord Sidmouth for making the lives of the prisoners in the county jail at Derby more comfortable, and then went for Locket, accusing him of arrogance displayed *'by this Method of Bribing the Witnesses wife's to come against us.'* He concluded:

"There hath existed a great deal of partiality to those who were more Implicated in the Affair and those who proposed the most Violent Measures who are at large and was not brought to trial – The business was magnified to such a degree by Mr Lockett that some should be sacrificed to satisfy him and others in their unjust proceedings for it was never known in England before that Labouring men were Tried for High Treason yea men who can Scarce tell a Letter in the alphabet"[68].

Apparently about half the prisoners were able, at the very least, to sign their names.

Life in Australia

On 20th October 1818, Thomas and his brother John were moved to the town of Winsor on the coaster 'General Hewitt'. During their first years in New South Wales, Tommy and his John lived in Windsor and then Parramatta. For part of their time they were assigned to the Rev Samuel Marsden, the Yorkshire parson who became a wealthy landowner and sheep breeder, probably as farm labourers on the Rooky Hill Estate, Melville. Thomas Bacon was logged as an invalid being both old and inform. John Bacon was granted a ticket of leave in June 1827, when he was living in the district of South Creek. He died in his early sixties in 1828 and was buried by Marsden at St John's Parramatta on 10th May.

As regards Thomas Bacon we need to make a few assumptions; he is absent from the 1819 Muster and the cumulative list of Rev Marsden's assignees of 1825 and also the 1825 Muster and 1828 Census. This suggests that he may have been at Port Macquarie from an early date and

---

[68] HO/40/10(1) quoted by Stevens, Op. Cit.

here we must assume that his age and infirmity precluded him from being a great deal of use as a labourer. Thomas Bacon was buried at Port Macquarie following a service by the Rev John Cross on 3rd July 1831 aged 77 and whilst still a prisoner. He had, apparently, been in failing health for some years.

Thomas Bacon had proved himself to be a careful man with a strong instinct for survival. It is not difficult to imagine him using his age and infirmity to obtain as easy a passage as possible.

There is no trace of Thomas communicating with his extensive family back in Britain.

21. Reflections of a Radical

Having read as much as I can uncover about our 'hero' Thomas Bacon, I feel I must now attempt the impossible. How would he reflect on his life, his experiences, his failures and his achievements? What would he choose to mark the high and low points of his long life?

As I sit in the scorching sun in this strange alien land I find my mind returning to what could have been, what should have been and what I have achieved, or more truthfully, failed to achieve. I have been quite ill of late, too poorly to work and I am, incidentally, the oldest convict in the region by some few years. I know my end is nigh. But it amazes me how I ever reached this age, particularly as no higher personage than Lord Sidmouth was after my head twenty or more years ago. I managed to escape that!

I'm writing from Port Macquarie in New South Wales, it is truly a million miles from Pentrich; it is a different world. It is a collection of shacks where old convicts, those who haven't been hanged, beaten to death, succumbed to strange diseases or even freed; come to die; that fate surely awaits me and soon.

Looking back to the trials I suppose I was lucky to endure transportation as Jeremiah Brandreth, Will Turner and Isaac Ludlam were hanged – unfairly in my view. They were convicted by a jury of property owners and farmers; how could they understand how we felt, how many of the jurors had faced starvation? How many would have recognised a frame if they had fallen over it?

I remain somewhat confused by George Weightman's reprieve. He is somewhere in this God forsaken land but I have not spoken to him in all these years. I always believed him to be a good man, as indeed was Isaac Ludlam. Although I had heard his reputation, I knew little of Brandreth before the dreadful events of that night.

The first thing I want to say is that I have always believed in reform, especially parliamentary reform. To begin with, by constitutional means but this proved hopeless. My declared intention was to work with the small number of middle and upper class men, men of quality, who were supposed to share our views, people like Major Cartwright, Sir Francis Burdett and writers like Thomas Paine, William Cobbett and others. However, it came to me that many of these well-heeled reformers were playing a game, a deadly game, but a game nevertheless. They were never going to raise a finger to take a risk, let alone take a life. We were never short of talkers, even of writers, but we had a great lack of leaders. Henry Hunt talked in flowery language but it were yellow daffodils

There were some good men in the midlands and the north; you know them as well as me. I never trusted the Londoners, too sharp, too posh with too much to lose!

I never wanted the Pentrich Rising to be our epitaph but that is what it turned out to be. It was never going to succeed, we lacked active support from influential people and, more to the point, we were duped by the government spy William Oliver; I hope he rots in hell!

Could I have stopped him, could I have warned the others, maybe? It was only towards the end that I realised Oliver was probably a spy. People were getting arrested, he were even arrested and let go. I started putting two and two together when he pressed us to change the date – I smelt a rat but I had no proof and many of the men were set on riot. It were difficult to get round to tell people.

Although I'd heard of Brandreth as an active radical, as I said I'd never knowingly met him until a couple a days before the Rising; there was nothing going to stop him, I could see that in his eyes straight away. So many delegates had promised men in great numbers but they began to drop out – Manchester lost interest, even Nottingham radicals were all talk! The brave men of Huddersfield got no further than we did. Many of them that were keen had been locked up after Habeas Corpus had been suspended.

How can one man stop a bull charging, even if it were that same man who provoked the bull in t' first place.

I could see no other option but to disappear so disappear I did. I tried to warn them in a roundabout way but they were all set to go.

So I hid in James Booth's hovel for a few days and then, John, me brother, and me set off. It wasn't to last we were sold in, I'm sure about that.

Some have asked me why I hid away, it sem't the right thing to do at the time, I were an old man, I couldn't walk to Nottingham, I'd have been a burden. I weren't a coward I've never bin a coward and I was never a turncoat. I didn't always tell the truth but I would not let colleagues down. Some did; Cope and Booth forb two!

The trial were a farce, they wanted to put on a show and, to begin with, I was top of the list, the first name. I had to take care of myself and, not having been on the march, I managed to get a deal by pleading guilty and keeping my head. I had to keep my counsel on Oliver but what could I have done? To be honest, I'd intended to bring Oliver into the reckoning but, was it worth me neck? I did think it might be worth taking the terrible drop. I knew they wanted me dead, what would you a done? Nobody told me I might a got away free.

From an early age, maybe as young as fifteen, I realised that my family were at the bottom of the tree. We lived from day to day. Our comfort and the food on our table was at the whim of the weather, the demand for whatever we had to sell (including our labour) and the landlord; in our case the Duke of Devonshire. No-one spoke for us, least of all the vicar; I decided I had to do something.

I took to reading like a duck to water; I read all I could get hold of – newspapers, pamphlets and the like. I used to pick them up in the bar of the Devonshire Inn, t'Anchor or t'Peacock. I even heard some men talking about the situation, the government, the mad King and what ought to be done.

I got invited to meetings, reform groups and the like. I began to travel to towns and cities most in Pentrich had even heard of. After a year or so I found the knowledge and confidence to speak myself. I found people listened and, often as not, agreed! That was how it all began and it were exciting, I'll not deny that.

As I read these scribbled notes I am forced to think whether I could I have done more, not more for myself – I did that – more for some of them Pentrich and South Wingfield men. Most of them were simple, uneducated and easily led particularly by elder relatives and hot-heads. For some, it were the best excitement they had ever had. A few had been soldiers but most had spent their entire lives within ten miles of where they were born.

I was involved in frame-breaking to protect the livelihoods of weavers in Pentrich, Swanwick and South Wingfield. I admit I even organised some of the raids but we never committed murder – I know as some did! After they made it a hanging job we gave up.

It was after that when people began talking about doing something much bigger to change the government. Petitions and talking were not working!

I had already been impressed by news of the French successes, reading Thomas Paine's papers and listening to Cobbett and others.

Did I do them any favours? Only time will tell and I don't think I have much of that.

Why did I plead 'guilty'? I often wonder. Cope, Martin and Booth had told lies trying to save their necks. There was a lot of bad practice, but what could I expect. I had put myself in the line and I don't regret it.

Many of the men were my friends, good friends and a good few were relatives. I feel bad about that, very bad.

So, that's it. I was never as bad as some said and, probably, never as good as I thought meself.

22. Conclusions

John Stevens' Concluding Comments

Before attempting to draw the ends together in may be useful to set out John Stevens' concluding comments as they relate to Thomas Bacon, whilst remembering that he was dealing with the Rising as an entity and all those involved at whatever stage or level.

"Thomas Bacon, that stockinger, with a 'degree of knowledge far beyond the attainment of men of his contition in life' – the author of this opinion (the solicitor Lockett) seems to have felt it improper for a framework knitter to educate himself – had been for many years the leader of the 'Pentrich political society'. He was also a leader in the wider conspiracy. According to a prosecution brief the village of Pentrich was chosen as one of the centres 'because it was the place of Birth and residence of the Prisoner Thomas Bacon . . . [and] within half a mile from the Turnpike and mail coach road between Sheffield and Birmingham . . .[69]

It was Bacon who gives details of the 'working class' make-up of the central committee which met at Wakefield on 5th May to discuss the Rising and hear a talk from 'The London Delegate', Oliver the Spy. All, the delegates – there were about 30 present – were men who, according to Bacon, 'worked hard for their Support and lived Hardly.' Only Oliver stood out from the others as 'a man of fashion'. Bacon spoke of Oliver as the *gentleman* reformer from London.

In Pentrich, old Bacon seems to have presided over a hotbed of sedition. His sister's public house, the White Horse, a meeting place of like minds, had a wide reputation. William Benbow, radical Manchester shoemaker, fiend of Cobbett and later a militant Chartist, attended a meeting there in December 1816, and it is interesting to note that when Benbow told the

---

[69] TS/11/132 quoted by Stevens, Op. Cit.

meeting that if they were steady, it could be done without bloodshed, it was a villager (unnamed) who said he hoped it would *not* be done without bloodshed, and he 'should like to kill himself three or four for Breakfast'[70].

This sort of bloodthirsty talk, born of desperate distress, would have found no sympathy from the more comfortable middle class men helping to lead the constitutional fight for universal suffrage.

How far the 'great men' were removed from the pikes and plots of the Midlands can be seen from London help for the penniless Derbyshire prisoners as they awaited trial. The London reformers told Hunt that it would be 'extremely improper' for them to identify themselves with 'house-breakers and murders' who had done 'the greatest injury to the cause of reform'.

Bacon's description of Oliver as a 'gentleman' was hardly accurate whatever meaning you put in that word. A two-faced builder recently out of debtors' prison, he nevertheless managed to cut a fine figure with his tall build, his ginger whiskers and his blue mixture pantaloons. But there is no need to introduce 'class' into the informing trade. Many agents were unemployed fellow workers.

How far did Midlands Luddism, concerned as it was with industrial protest, have links and threads with political agitation? It is hardly likely that the two movements were entirely separate, and very likely that the individual members of one activity had connections with the other. Again Thomas Bacon is a key figure. The authorities suspected him of having been a Luddite – 'in the year 1812 he was head of the Luddite party in Pentrich and Swanwick which did considerable mischief in those places.

A puzzle of immediate interest to the Pentrich Affair is how Thomas Bacon escaped the gallows. Brandreth was so important a figure – he was a last-minute fortuitous choice to lead the villagers – but he killed a man and the 'general' on the day so he could expect to be hanged. Without Bacon,

---

[70] TS/11/132 quoted by Stevens, Op. Cit.

however, who can believe that villagers from what was then the 'back of beyond' would have taken it upon themselves to tackle Lord Liverpool's government. The government knew he was the chief man, and first intended to arraign him as the most important conspirator – 'The King against Thomas Bacon'; the observer at the trial was of the same opinion: '. . . Thomas Bacon . . .was ringleader and mover of the plot & deserved hanging most richly'. And George Goodwin, the ironworks manager who knew most of the men involved repeated this view: 'Thos. Bacon of Pentrich is the great ringleader.' Yet he escaped with his life. The reason often assumed – that Bacon escaped with transportation because he did not take part in the march – seems thin; though his absence on the day is another puzzle.

Oliver may be the key. Was Thomas Bacon, the 'Nestor of the Derbyshire reformers', put down the list because. Whereas it is unlikely that Brandreth met the spy, Bacon met Oliver at the important Wakefield meeting of 5th May, and would have dragged all that up in court?

Thank you Mr Stevens.

If one takes the Pentrich Rising as the overriding feature of Thomas Bacon's life then it is easy to classify it as a disappointment and, of course, a total failure. Looking at the Pentrich Rising from a detached position it amounts to little more than a few hours of madness achieving absolutely nothing. More to the point, for some of the marchers it cost them their heads, for others their liberty and for some escaping formal justice, their homes and livelihoods. Many lived in houses of or in the service of the Duke of Devonshire who took a distinctly unfavourable view of this type of behaviour. The sentences handed down were harsh and, at the lower end, disproportionate to the actual involvement of some. This said I believe that many of those engaged, other than those 'pressed' by family, neighbours and stronger minds, believed they had a case and that a revolution was the only way to change things. They were actively encouraged in this belief not only by fervent but misguided men; they were encouraged by a government sponsored agent provocateur whose motivation was pecuniary rather than one of principle; William Oliver 'the spy'.

However, the Rising was a small step along a path that did eventually arrive at universal male suffrage later in the same century, a limited representative voice and the freedom for workers to combine together in order to improve their situation.

There is an alternative perspective and that is the one observed from Westminster. They effectively squashed a rebellion with little effort (a few well-placed spies and less than two dozen soldiers), they put on a show trial that would, and did, make others consider their actions and, whilst they did not manage to hang Thomas Bacon, they had three severed heads to display and had managed to dispose of an irritant of many years standing. The Rising was used as justification for a series of six oppressive acts of parliament passed after the trial, see chapter twelve.

It is ironic to add that Thomas Bacon's aim of parliamentary reform, if he was not to gain a 'republic', was partially fulfilled by the Reform Act 1832; the year after his death. The 'republican state' is no closer and probably never will be.

It should be mentioned that that Reform Act 1832 did not please all; many people were disappointed. Voting in the boroughs was restricted to men who occupied homes with an annual value of £10. There were also property qualifications for people living in rural areas. As a result, only one in seven adult males had the vote. Nor were the constituencies of equal size. Whereas 35 constituencies had less than 300 electors, Liverpool had a constituency of over 11,000. I doubt Thomas Bacon would have been satisfied!

Although a considerable amount is known about his activities, there are many unanswered questions surrounding the life of Thomas Bacon. For example:

1. Whilst it is undoubtedly true that throughout his life he consistently sought parliamentary reform. Did he ever want this to be achieved by peaceful means such as petitioning the government, negotiation and argument or was he always favouring reform by insurrection and violent revolution?
2. Why did he fail to take part in and lead the Pentrich Rising?
3. He was an influential man, if he did suspect Oliver to be a spy, why didn't he make more efforts to dissuade the marchers, most of whom were his family, friends and neighbours?
4. Did he ever visit America, as many writers suggest; but they do so without providing any evidence?

Edward Thompson (1968), in quoting the prosecution brief[71] says, even without Oliver's patent provocations, some kind of insurrection would probably have been attempted, and perhaps with a greater measure of success. Indeed, in the Crown's view, not Oliver nor Mitchell, but Thomas Bacon, who himself travelled between Nottingham, Derby, Yorkshire, Lancashire and Birmingham, was the main instigator of rebellion. If this is true, and there is a degree of corroboration, why did he fail to attend the Rising? Why did he not appear at what could have been his 'finest hour'.

A further element of the Pentrich Rising identified[72] by Thompson was that he saw it " . . . as one of the first attempts in history to mount a wholly proletarian insurrection without middle class support".

White[73] suggests that many of the radicals active in the period immediately post-1817 regarded Luddism, hunger-marches, and the adventures of Jeremiah Brandreth as futile irrelevancies, implying that formal

---

[71] Thompson, E.P. *"The Making of the English Working Class"* Penguin (1968) p. 735 quoting *"The King v Thomas Bacon"* brief in Treasury Solicitors 11.351. and Home Office 52.172
[72] Thompson, Op. Cit.
[73] White, Op. Cit.

parliamentary pressure is more likely to bring about parliamentary reform; maybe they were right!

Thomas Bacon was not the only working class radical by any means but he did play a significant role in movement over the period 1780 to 1817. What were his achievements? What were his mistakes? Does he deserve a role in radical history? Was he used by middle-class radicals and reformers to do what they did not wish to undertake themselves?

One of the questions unanswered in this sad story is 'why Pentrich?' A prosecution brief was to suggest that the village of Pentrich was chosen as a suitable venue for the Rising, and the government 'set-up', was that it was the home and operating base of one of their main targets, Thomas Bacon. In a postscript to his evidence at the trials, George Goodwin, the manager at Butterley Company, named the name he believed was behind the trouble, "Thomas Bacon is the great ringleader."

Finally, I return to the four questions posed a little earlier:

1. Whilst it is undoubtedly true that throughout his life he consistently sought parliamentary reform. Did he ever want this to be achieved by peaceful means such as petitioning the government, negotiation and argument or was he always favouring reform by open revolution?

I believe that the evidence, circumstantial as much of it is, proves that Thomas Bacon was always a 'republican'. He firmly believed that the ruling class would never relinquish their power unless forced to do so. One change Bacon would not have seen quite so clearly in the early nineteenth century was the advancement of the 'Merchant Princes' and the new industrialists into the power structure.

2. Why did he fail to take part in and lead the Pentrich Rising?

The evidence that seems to me to be most reliable is that given in the statements as he began his journey and during his transportation. Why would he lie then? In addition, it must have been a factor in Bacon's decision that he was not physically capable of such as escapade. He did visit Nottingham seeking an alternative leader, eventually introducing Brandreth to the men at Pentrich and South Wingfield.

I think the circumstantial evidence supports the fact that the warrant was issued after the Rising and not before 9th June.

However, I cannot avoid reaching the conclusion that he anticipated a disaster and he was 'looking after his own neck'!

> 3. He was an influential man, if he did suspect Oliver to be a spy, why didn't he make more efforts to dissuade the marchers, most of whom were his family, friends and neighbours?

He doubtless developed a mistrust of Oliver sometime in late May early June 1817. He tried to warn William Stevens of Nottingham but was rejected. Why was his concerns taken seriously; was Stevens involved in the plan to ambush the Pentrich Rising? Communicating with diverse groups, separate villages and key people would also have been a severe constraint on any efforts to warn others.

> 4. Did he ever visit America, as many writers suggest; but they do so without providing any evidence?

There seems to me to be no evidence whatsoever that Bacon ever visited America. Whether he said he had made this trip to bolster his credibility - his 'CV' - or others merely repeated this unsupported 'fact' until it became 'accepted' as true is possible.

Thomas Bacon was different from his peers his driving force was intense and more considered than that of the others at his social level. Had he lived 100 years later we may well have seen him hold a position of power and influence in a socialist party or a trade union representing working class views.

Whilst he did not seem to possess a likeable personality, he was doubtless an intriguing and intelligent man. He was the instigator of the Pentrich Rising and, for me, as integral a part as was Jeremiah Brandreth, if not even more so. He deserves to be remembered and to join the list of Derbyshire notables.

Bibliography

Feiling, Keith (1950) *"A History of England"* Book Club Associates

Halevy, Elie *"A History of the English People in the nineteenth Century"* Ernest Benn Ltd, London (1924) Abacas, London

Hobsbawn, Eric (1962) "The Age of Revolution 1789 – 1848" Weidenfield and Nicholson

Hopkins, Eric (1979) *"A Social History of the English Working Class"* Edward Arnold, London

Macaulay, Thomas Babington (1848) *"The History of England"*

Neal, John, (1966) "The Pentrich Revolution" Pentrich Church Restoration Committee (originally published as newspaper articles in 1895

Pike, E. Royston (1966) *"Human Documents of the Industrial Revolution in Britain"* George Allen & Unwin Ltd 1966

Porter, Roy, "English Society in the Eighteenth Century" Penguin (1982)

Report of the Proceedings including The Trails of Jeremiah Brandreth and others for High Treason, etc. printed by Sutton & Son, Bridlesmith Gate, Derby

Royle, Edward "Radical Politics 1790-1900 Religion and Unbelief" Longman (1971)

Stevens, John, (1977) *"England's Last Revolution"* Moorland Publishing, Buxton

Thompson, E.P. "The Making of the English Working Class" Pub. Penguin (1968)

White, R.J. *"Waterloo to Peterloo"* pub. Mercury Books London, (1963)

Index

"Address to Journeymen and Labourers" by William Cobbett 29, 45
Addington, Henry, see Sidmouth
"Age of Reason" by Thomas Paine 26
Alfreton, Derbyshire 13, 67
Allens, Thomas 67
Ambergate, Derbyshire 97
America 8, 24, 50, 52, 64
American War of Independence 24, 25, 83, 84
Anchor Inn, Oakerthorpe 22, 42, 149
Annual General Elections 74
Apprentices 16
Arkwright, Sir Richard 43, 55, 61
Asherfield Farm and barn 106, 117
Astor, Nancy MP 83
Bacon, John, brother of Thomas 12, 121, 139
Bamford, Samuel 34, 36, 46, 66, 113, 131
Barnes, James 116
Bastille, attack in Paris 32, 76, 85
Bell Inn, London 63
Belper, Derbyshire 97
Benbow, William 28, 35-36, 151
Binns, John 64-65
Birmingham 19, 41, 107, 116, 118, 132
"Black Dwarf" by Thomas Wooler 10, 36, 46, 66, 105
Blanketeers 35, 47, 113, 115
Bonaparte, Napoleon 85
Booth, Armond 106, 108, 140
Booth, James 120, 148
Bow Street Runners 61
Brandreth, Jeremiah 7, 16, 47, 58, 70, 99, 107, 118, 121, 123, 125-126, 128-129, 138, 147, 155
Brassington, George 118, 144
Brettle & Ward, Belper 16

Brighton Pavilion 71
Brummell, George 'Beau' 71
Brunswick family 118-119
Buckland Hollow, Derbyshire 14, 15, 120
Bunyan, John, author 23, 42, 47
Burdett, Sir Francis 34, 68, 74-75, 78, 81, 106, 116, 148
Burke, Edmund 26-27, 63, 85
Butterley Company 19, 44, 45, 74, 106, 115, 118, 122, 127, 156
Buxton, German 144
Byron, Lord 2, 93
Cartwright, Major John 23, 30, 31-34, 46, 64-66, 68, 72, 78, 80-81, 148, 150
Castle, the spy 76
Catholic Emancipation 24, 73
Cato Street Conspiracy 40, 64, 95
Cavandish, William, see Devonshire
Chatsworth House, Derbyshire 14
Cheese Riots, Nottingham 55
Chief Baron, see Richards
Cobbett, William 28-31, 35, 47, 68, 74, 81, 151
Cochrane, Lord 68, 80, 116
Cock and Mulberry Inn, London 75
Cock Inn, Ripley 42, 67
Codnor, Derbyshire 128
Coke, Daniel, MP 88
'Common Sense' pamphlet by Thomas Paine 25
Condorcet 25
Cope, John 45, 107, 111-112, 115, 122, 140
Corn Laws 93
'Crisis' papers 25
Crabtree, George 70, 116, 118
Cross, Rev John 146
Crown and Anchor, London 31, 34, 78 – 82
Denham, Thomas QC, defence barrister 138
Derby 104, 125
Derby Mercury 22

Derby Silk Mill 4
Derbyshire Delegate 45
Derbyshire Advertiser 114
Derbyshire Rib 16-17
Desmoulin, Camille 76
Devonshire, Duke of 12, 14, 61, 98, 153
Devonshire Inn, Buckland Hollow 22, 42
Directory of France 85
Disturbances 8, 57, 89, 92
Dog and Partridge Inn, Middleton 113
Dog Inn, Pentrich 12
Eastwood, Nottinghamshire 129
Eaton, Derby Jailer 142
Enclosures 12
Fawcett, Millicent 100
'Feelosafers' 31, 45
Fielding, Henry, novelist 61
Fitton, William 66
Fox, Charles John 85
Framework Knitters 16-17
Franklin, Benjamin 25, 54
French Horn Inn, Codnor 128
French Revolution 7, 23, 25, 27, 41, 44, 48, 71, 72, 77, 85
Frost, John 63 - 64
Gagging Acts 37, 77, 89 95
General Hewitt, Australian coaster 145
George II 83
George III 25, 65, 73, 83, 84, 90
George IV (see Prince Regent)
Giltbrook, Nottinghamshire 128
Glasshouse Inn, Codnor 128
Glorious Revolution 23
Godber, Josiah 144
Golden Fleece Pub, Nottingham 105
Goodwin, George 19, 127-128, 139, 156
Goose Fair, Nottingham 55

Gordon Riots 24
Grand Jury 142
Grey, Charles 46, 86
Habeas Corpus 28, 38, 88, 148
Halton, Col. Wingfield JP 126
Hampden Clubs 33, 34, 35, 46, 65
Hampden Club, Birmingham 33
Hampden Club, Heanor 67
Hampden Club, Nottingham 105
Hampden Club, Pentrich 13, 67
Hampden, John 65
Hansard 28
Hardy, Thomas 63, 86
Hargreaves, James 55
Haslam, Edward 106
Haynes, Samuel 106, 115
Healey, Joseph 66
Heanor, Derbyshire 67, 125
Henson, Gravener 37-39, 143
Hepworth, Mrs Mary 99, 126
High Sheriff 60-62
High Treason 40, 135-136
Horne, William 30
House of Commons 68
Huddersfield 19, 33, 49, 66, 122, 125, 144, 148
Huddersfield Local History Society 131
Hunt, Daniel 126
Hunt, Henry 'Orator' 33, 47, 74, 75, 80, 148, 152
Hussars 128
"IKEA" 128
Impressment 51
Income Tax 73
Infant Mortality 13
Irish 'Problem' 84
Jacobinism 7, 47, 89
Jenkinson, Robert (see Lord Liverpool)

Joyce, William 137
Justices of the Peace 61
Kay, John 55
Laissez-faire 71
Langley Mill, Derbyshire 128
"Letter to the Luddites" by William Cobbett 29
Life Expectancy 19
Liverpool, Lord 71, 94, 153
Lockett, William, prosecution solicitor 108, 135, 144, 145
Lombe, John 4
London Corresponding Society 63-66, 86
Lord Haw Haw, see Joyce
Lord Lieutenant 60
Louis XVI 85
Luddites 20, 38, 39, 44, 50-59, 86, 92, 152, 155
Ludlam, Isaac (Elder) 7, 49, 70, 72, 138, 142, 147
Magna Carta 89
Manchester 19, 33, 35, 105, 125, 148
Marsden, Rev Samuel 145
Master Hosier 16
Methodism 15, 22, 48, 49, 73
Metropolitan Police 61
Mining 15
Mitchell, Joseph 81, 82, 104, 105, 131
Nadin, Joseph 34
Nags Head, Heanor 74
Napoleonic Wars 33, 66, 67
Naval Mutiny 90
Nestor of Derbyshire 20, 46, 153
Newgate Prison 142
New Inn, Codnor 128
Newark, Nottinghamshire 125
Northmore, Thomas 65
Nottingham 19, 37, 55, 125, 128, 148
'Nottingham Captain', see Brandreth
Nottingham Secret Committee 70, 103

Oakerthorpe, Derbyshire 14
Oliver, William 'The Spy' 33, 62, 70, 101, 104, 106, 113, 121-122, 128, 131-134, 136, 140, 143, 144, 148, 149, 151, 152, 154, 157
Onion, John 107, 115
Orders in Council 87
Paine, Thomas 23, 24-26, 41, 54, 85, 148, 150
Pankhurst, Emmeline 100
Parramatta, Australia 145
Peacock Inn, Oakerthorpe 14, 22, 42, 149
Peel, Sir Robert 91
Pentrich, Derbyshire 11, 13, 15, 58, 67, 98, 106, 130, 149, 150, 152, 156
Perceval, Spencer 73
Peterloo Massacre 34, 36
Phillips, Captain Hussars 129
'*Pilgrim's Progress*' by John Bunyan 23, 42, 47
Pitt the Younger, William 84
"*Political Register*" William Cobbett's newspaper 28
Port Macquarie 146, 147
Press Gangs 56
Preston, George JP 114
Prince Regent 56, 71, 73, 74, 75, 94, 102, 103
Privy Council 87
Radical – definition 30
Radical, definition 3
Reform Act 1832 153
Reign of Terror 48
'Retribution' Prison Hulk 142
Richards, Richard, KC (Chief Baron) 137, 138
Richards, W.T., see Oliver
'*Rights of Man*' by Thomas Paine 23, 25, 43, 47, 68
Ripley, Derbyshire 11, 13, 67, 125, 128
Robertson, Talbot Inn 104
Rochdale 66
Rolleston, Launcelot JP 129
Saint Monday 18
Secret Ballots 74

Secret Committees 58, 69, 77
Seditious Meetings Act 35
Seven Year War 83
Sidmouth, Lord 77, 93, 103, 105
Sheffield 9, 104, 104, 132
'Shiners' 16
Smith, Abraham 105, 106
Smith, William 106, 107
Society for Constitutional Reform 32
South Creek, Parramatta, Australia 145
South Wingfield, Derbyshire 11-14, 44, 18, 20, 22, 23, 25, 44-45, 59, 70, 82, 98, 101, 120, 126, 130, 150, 157
Spa Fields Riots, 74, 75
Spence, Thomas 39, 75, 134
Spenceans 75
Spence's Plan 39
St George's Fields Massacre 24
St Ives, Huntingdon 135
St Matthew's Church, Pentrich 11
St John's, Parramatta 145
Stamp Act 1765 27
Stevens, William 70, 113, 143, 144, 157
Suffragette Movement 100
Sun Inn, Eastwood, Nottinghamshire 129
Swanwick, Derbyshire 11, 13, 18, 42, 56, 97, 106, 127, 150, 152
Sydney, Australia 143
"Take Your Choice" by Major Cartwright 23, 32
Talbot Inn, Derby 63, 104
Tambora, Mount 73
Thelwall, John 64, 89
The Times 22
Thistlewood, Anthony 64, 75
Three Salmons, Nottingham 70
'Tottenham' Convict Ship 9, 143
Tolpuddle Martyrs 90
Tuppenny Trash 28, 29, 45

Turner, William 7, 70, 72, 99, 138, 142, 144, 147
Turpin, Dick 14
Universal Suffrage 74
Wakefield 104, 105, 132, 151
Walters, Robert 128
Watson, Dr James 75
Watson, James jnr 75, 76
Weightman, George 70, 106,125, 128, 129, 138, 140, 147
Weightman, Joseph 106, 108
Weightman, Nancy 13, 20, 72, 99,123,140
Weightman, Nathaniel 107
Weightman, William 128
Wesley, John 15, 48
Weston, Samuel 67
White Horse Inn, Pentrich 12, 13, 22, 42, 44, 98, 108, 151
Wilkes, John 24
Wilson, Sir Robert 116
Wolstenholme, Rev Hugh 72, 105
Wolstenholme, William 105, 132
Wollstonecraft, Mary 100
Wooler, Thomas 30, 36-37, 105
Wyld, John 106
Wyvill, Rev Christopher 64

Made in the USA
Charleston, SC
03 February 2015